Most readers would be amazed that a had enough life experiences to accrue "Amazing," however, is the description of Ashley herself! This memoir is an account of an ongoing celebration of life, not in terms solely of events, but in terms of spirit!

--Beverly Slaughter,
Provost/Honors Program Director,
Eastern Florida State College, Cocoa, FL

This is an uplifting and compelling book of survival and achievement in the face of tremendous adversity. This brave and courageous young woman is describing the indescribable without bitterness or self-pity. Ashley McGrath speaks as often of her joys in life as her challenges in a refreshingly open, frank and unbiased manner.

--Roxanne Guy, M.D., F.A.C.S.,
Past President of the American Society of Plastic Surgeons

A moving account of the struggle for survival. Ashley McGrath is humble about her own positive attitude and determination to have a fulfilling life, despite a genetic disorder and serious related medical issues. Her life story holds a message for each of us.

--Valerie Allen, Ed.D., Psychologist and
Co-Founder of Authors for Authors

You will love and cheer Ashley through her captivating stories as much as those of us who are blessed enough to call her our friend. You'll be ashamed the next time you complain about your minor obstacles. This is no whining, woe-is-me account by a handicapped woman.

--Linda Jump, Author and Photographer

An inspirational story with lessons in determination and perseverance for all of us.
--Donnice Stephenson, English Department Chair
Bayside High School, Palm Bay, FL

UnabASHed by Disability:
An Autobiography

by
Ashley M. McGrath

Acknowledgments

I hereby express my gratitude to the following people:

- My writing mentor Joyce Good Henderson and her company Faith's Loom Books for making the publication of this book possible. Thank you for your guidance and friendship, Joyce.
- My parents Marty and Tracy McGrath, who made me the person I am today through their devoted care. They also helped me fill in the blanks about my childhood for this book.
- Local author and photographer Linda Jump, who provided me with valuable information about how to write a memoir and reviewed this book.
- My cousin Ann Rooney Heuer, also a published author, for reviewing each chapter of my book and for her support.
- My high school English teacher Donnice Stephenson for copy editing the manuscript and for her review.
- Other individuals who reviewed my autobiography: Beverly Slaughter, Dr. Roxanne Guy, Dr. Valerie Allen, Dr. John Opitz, Dr. Jurgen Spranger, and Trish Hebert.
- My Uncle James McGrath, who took the photos located on the front and back covers.
- God for giving me life, for the strength to go through tough times, and for providing me with the words for my autobiography.
- Everyone else who had a part in my life (especially my grandparents) and in the publication of this book.

Contents

Foreword

Ashley McGrath's beautiful and moving monograph deserves the careful and respectful attention of all with a more than passing interest in the *condition humaine* written not as something imagined, say by Honoré Balzac or Charles Dickens, but as lived today by a real flesh-and-blood person about herself and the condition she was born with, indeed conceived with. The "all" mentioned above must include not only readers at large, but especially the professionals involved in the study of and entrusted with the care of individuals with a congenital anomaly, syndrome, or other genetic disorder uncommon in the general population, but a challenge to those who must know and to those who must live with these conditions.

The particular condition of Ashley McGrath, the campomelic syndrome, was initially designated *syndrome campomelique* by Pierre Maroteaux of Paris in 1971, an expert on skeletal dysplasias whose facility with Greek and Latin allowed him to coin apt and mellifluous terms for congenital anomalies of the skeleton - here meaning curved, not crooked. Note also that the initial designation was campomelic *syndrome*, not dysplasia as if it affected the skeleton alone, as serious as the occasional camptomelic one encounters there also, historically to be attributed to the later an apparent attempt to claim priority.

The concept of syndrome comes vividly alive in Ashley's tale, so, please pay careful attention to the various organs or parts of her body that are involved *pleiotropically*, which means: multiply, due to a single cause, in this case a mutation in the ancient gene *SOX-9*.

Ashley's story must also be of compelling interest to the genetic counselors who will all, sooner or later, see someone in hospital or clinic with her condition.

A Primer on *Campomelic Syndrome*

My life has been affected the most by a genetic disorder called *campomelic syndrome*, also known as campomelic dysplasia or dwarfism, which interferes with development of the skeleton and reproductive system.

The term *campomelic* (also spelled *camptomelic*) is derived from Greek words that mean "bent limb." Individuals with *campomelic syndrome* typically have bowing in the long bones in their legs and sometimes in their arms, resulting in skin dimples over curved bones. They also tend to have short legs, dislocated hips, underdeveloped shoulder blades, eleven pairs of ribs (as opposed to twelve), neck bone abnormalities, and clubfeet.

Other features of *campomelic syndrome* include a small chin, prominent eyes, a flat face, and a large head compared to the body. This disorder also shares characteristics of Pierre Robin sequence: a cleft palate (an opening in the roof of the mouth), glossoptosis (a tongue located farther back than usual), and micrognathia (a small lower jaw).

Many people with *campomelic syndrome* have ambiguous genitalia and reproductive organs that are not consistent with their sex. For example, I have a typical male chromosome pattern (46, XY) but have female reproductive organs, so I was officially identified as a female at birth and have lived my life thus.

Campomelic syndrome is caused by mutations in or near the *SOX9* gene on chromosome 17, which gives directions on how to make a protein that helps form many tissues and organs during an embryo's development. If this protein fails to regulate other genes that develop the skeleton and reproductive organs, signs of *campomelic syndrome* appear.

Campomelic syndrome is inherited in an autosomal dominant pattern, meaning that one copy of the altered *SOX9* gene in each cell can lead to this disorder. The disorder is diagnosed by genetic specialists and most frequently happens in individuals with no family history of the disorder. *Campomelic syndrome* is relatively rare, occurring from one in 40,000 to 200,000 births, according to estimates by the National Institute of Health.

Foreword

Ashley McGrath's beautiful and moving monograph deserves the careful and respectful attention of all with a more than passing interest in the *condition humaine* written not as something imagined, say by Honoré Balzac or Charles Dickens, but as lived today by a real flesh-and-blood person about herself and the condition she was born with, indeed conceived with. The "all" mentioned above must include not only readers at large, but especially the professionals involved in the study of and entrusted with the care of individuals with a congenital anomaly, syndrome, or other genetic disorder uncommon in the general population, but a challenge to those who must know and to those who must live with these conditions.

The particular condition of Ashley McGrath, the campomelic syndrome, was initially designated *syndrome campomelique* by Pierre Maroteaux of Paris in 1971, an expert on skeletal dysplasias whose facility with Greek and Latin allowed him to coin apt and mellifluous terms for congenital anomalies of the skeleton - here meaning curved, not crooked. Note also that the initial designation was campomelic *syndrome*, not dysplasia as if it affected the skeleton alone, as serious as the occasional camptomelic one encounters there also, historically to be attributed to the later an apparent attempt to claim priority.

The concept of syndrome comes vividly alive in Ashley's tale, so, please pay careful attention to the various organs or parts of her body that are involved *pleiotropically*, which means: multiply, due to a single cause, in this case a mutation in the ancient gene *SOX-9*.

Ashley's story must also be of compelling interest to the genetic counselors who will all, sooner or later, see someone in hospital or clinic with her condition.

Her condition, the campomelic syndrome, having early on acquired a nasty reputation in our field due to the complexity, multiplicity, severity and yes, even lethality of the most severely affected who therefore, were called to the attention of clinicians much earlier than the mildly affected survivors - some even without the characteristic Middleton triad: 1. Anterior bowing of the tibia between its lower one-third and upper two thirds with 2. overlying skin dimple and 3. associated club foot, including some with straight legs.

An opportunity again of impressing on parents and family of an affected child that the campomelic syndrome is not a curable disease, but a *condition*, a chronic, lifelong state-of-being. A state of being which, of course, shapes more or less strongly the personality and lifestyle of the person so affected. Best outcomes being those in which all professionals, parents and families involved adopt early, as soon as the infant is out of danger, an attitude of "God makes no junk" and "we are looking at a potential champion in the Special Olympics" or spelling bees, or musical and intellectual endeavors and training.

We also want all support groups, especially those with a genetic focus to pay attention to Ashley's memoir. It begs not pity or compassion, but commands our highest admiration and respect for Ashley's successfully courageous confrontation with her condition; we wish that many able-bodied folks had as much gumption and spunk.

Ashley's story, unique as it is now, joins an ever-increasing number of such recollections by "patients" and/or parents dealing with many different conditions, written with different degrees of passion, but *all* offering numerous examples of personal, medical, social, educational, institutional hurdles overcome successfully in one way or another. What moves readers of these accounts to utter astonishment is the truly remarkable absence of self-pity. Rather, it is the ingenuity, resourcefulness, will and determination which enabled the affected, perhaps hurting in body and soul, to succeed frequently at all odds, to redeem their suffering, to bestow meaning on their existence, and to get on with life toward a goal of self-determination, self-affirmation, and ultimate compensation for losses, or for structures and functions they never had.

As such, better than any novelist, these strong and inspired persons, patients, men, women, young or old, in their accounts to us and our generation, offer something essential it lacks so often - namely hope.

These accounts, like Ashley McGrath's, define the meaning of courage and show us the means to increase pleasure at existence, promote survival and successfully turn joy into real happiness, tears into smiles, smiles into life-laughter.

Consequently, we are instructed that life is infinitely more complex, diverse and more beautiful than we, born intact, could have ever imagined.

And for that we owe Ashley McGrath a profound debt of gratitude.

John M. Opitz, MD
Professor of Pediatrics (Medical Genetics)
University of Utah, Salt Lake City

Jürgen W. Spranger, MD
Emeritus Professor of Pediatrics
University of Mainz, Germany

Reference: Maroteaux P, Spranger JW, Opitz JM, Kučera J, Lowry RB, Schimke RN, Kagan SM. 1971. Le syndrome campomélique. Presse Méd 79:1157-1162.

A Primer on *Campomelic Syndrome*

My life has been affected the most by a genetic disorder called *campomelic syndrome*, also known as campomelic dysplasia or dwarfism, which interferes with development of the skeleton and reproductive system.

The term *campomelic* (also spelled *camptomelic*) is derived from Greek words that mean "bent limb." Individuals with *campomelic syndrome* typically have bowing in the long bones in their legs and sometimes in their arms, resulting in skin dimples over curved bones. They also tend to have short legs, dislocated hips, underdeveloped shoulder blades, eleven pairs of ribs (as opposed to twelve), neck bone abnormalities, and clubfeet.

Other features of *campomelic syndrome* include a small chin, prominent eyes, a flat face, and a large head compared to the body. This disorder also shares characteristics of Pierre Robin sequence: a cleft palate (an opening in the roof of the mouth), glossoptosis (a tongue located farther back than usual), and micrognathia (a small lower jaw).

Many people with *campomelic syndrome* have ambiguous genitalia and reproductive organs that are not consistent with their sex. For example, I have a typical male chromosome pattern (46, XY) but have female reproductive organs, so I was officially identified as a female at birth and have lived my life thus.

Campomelic syndrome is caused by mutations in or near the *SOX9* gene on chromosome 17, which gives directions on how to make a protein that helps form many tissues and organs during an embryo's development. If this protein fails to regulate other genes that develop the skeleton and reproductive organs, signs of *campomelic syndrome* appear.

Campomelic syndrome is inherited in an autosomal dominant pattern, meaning that one copy of the altered *SOX9* gene in each cell can lead to this disorder. The disorder is diagnosed by genetic specialists and most frequently happens in individuals with no family history of the disorder. *Campomelic syndrome* is relatively rare, occurring from one in 40,000 to 200,000 births, according to estimates by the National Institute of Health.

Babies with this disorder are born with laryngotracheomalacia, weak cartilage in the upper respiratory tract. This condition blocks the airway and makes breathing difficult for infants, sometimes causing death.

If children with *campomelic syndrome* survive infancy, they will probably have scoliosis (a curvature of the spine) and other spine abnormalities that compress the spinal cord, a short stature, hearing loss, and low to normal intelligence.

Most of the above describes me physically in a nutshell. The rest of this book shows how I have lived with *campomelic syndrome*.

Here are helpful websites about *campomelic syndrome*:

- http://ghr.nlm.nih.gov/condition/campomelic-dysplasia (Genetics Home Reference, National Library of Medicine)
- http://www.aboutkidshealth.ca/En/HealthAZ/ConditionsandDiseases/GeneticDisorders/Pages/campomelic-dysplasia.aspx (AboutKidsHealth)
- http://www.lpaonline.org/assets/documents/NH%20Campmelic%20Dysplasia1.pdf (Little People of America)

Preface

Although there are challenges to living with physical disabilities, I'm thankful for growing up during a period of increasing understanding and acceptance of individuals with handicaps in the United States. I know the Americans with Disabilities Act of 1990 has made my life better, and I look forward to seeing how much better life will be for people with disabilities in the future.

In the past, a few people have told me I should write a book about my life. I didn't seriously consider doing this until shortly before my twenty-fifth birthday when I found myself being more reflective about my life since I had lived a quarter of a century. Having completed my Master's degree, I had adequate time to devote to writing. I worked on this book irregularly over the past three years and eventually attended a memoir writing class. The class combined with the passing of my maternal grandfather at the end of 2012 gave me the motivation I needed to finish my autobiography. The completion of this book is one of my proudest accomplishments.

People with disabilities and their loved ones as well as the general public would benefit from reading my autobiography. I think everyone should consider writing his or her life story, whether it's published or not. This allows you to reflect on your life and perhaps to set additional goals you'd like to achieve. A written record of your life is an invaluable gift for your descendants.

If you have a question or would like to leave a comment, please feel free to email me at AshMarMcG@aol.com. You can also find me on LinkedIn, Facebook, and Twitter (@AshMarMcG).

I hope you'll enjoy reading my life story.

Ashley M. McGrath
Palm Bay, Florida
September 2014

Introduction

I remember meeting Ashley for the first time. She and my son were in the same kindergarten class, and I saw her when I dropped him off for his first day in the class. There was something about Ashley that struck me immediately, and it had nothing to do with her wheelchair or adaptive communication device. It was the joy that absolutely radiated from her. I saw a happy, friendly, outgoing little girl eager to interact with the world.

An event in her early teens exemplifies Ashley's life. In her eighth grade year I was attending an award ceremony at which my son received an academic award. Although I don't remember much of the program, one presentation stands out clearly in my mind. Having already sat through numerous awards presentations, people began to get restless as the Principal started to extol the virtues of yet another student. It wasn't much different from all the previous awards, except for one thing. The list of accomplishments and achievements seemed never-ending; from volunteering at her church to being a member of the 4-H Club, this student was involved in everything!

I recall wondering how in the world any *kid* could possibly do so much and still have time to attend school. And how any *parent* could keep up with a schedule like that! By the end of the list, everyone wanted to know the identity of this extraordinary child. Sure enough, the student was none other than Ashley! I have come to realize over the past twenty years, that while all those accomplishments would be extraordinary for the typical child, it was the norm for Ashley.

Ashley's extraordinary life is one of grace. It is with awe that I watch this remarkable young woman live her life in faith, hope and love as a writer, mentor, lector, even poker player. I know from watching her that she truly is capable of accomplishing whatever she sets her mind and heart toward. She packs more into a year than most of us will in a lifetime.

As she goes through life, Ashley lives every day with utmost kindness, generosity and grace. I have much to learn from her.

Trish Hebert
Family friend

Chapter 1

Iffy Infancy

"Ashley might not live to see her first birthday;
if she does, she may be mentally challenged."

A child with special needs was completely unexpected when my mom and dad found out in the summer of 1985 they were going to be parents. The series of events that led to my birth began with a class my mother, Tracy Jensen, and my father, Marty McGrath, took at a community college outside of Buffalo, New York, in the late 1970s. Little did they know their parents had already met at my great-grandfather Joseph Jensen's retirement party a decade earlier. While holding the door open for her, my dad couldn't help but notice my mom and her beautiful smile along with a neck brace she wore due to a minor car accident.

My parents' chance meeting led to a life together, as they dated for a few years before getting married on August 22, 1981. A few months later, my mom was diagnosed with a condition that can cause infertility.

An Unusual Baby Story

My parents moved to Melbourne, Florida, in the spring of 1984. That fall, they bought a house in Palm Bay and became established in their careers. Two years later, Mom retired from her government secretarial position during the Reagan administration so she could focus on being a mother. Dad had a good job as a mechanical engineer, making my parents' decision to live on one income easier.

Pregnancy wasn't too difficult for Mom, but she had moderate morning sickness for the first trimester. As her pregnancy progressed, she occasionally felt my foot or elbow poke her inside near her belly button. An ultrasound revealed I had an unusually large head. My lack of movement concerned Mom and Dad, but they wouldn't know until my birth what was wrong with their baby.

On the evening of Saturday, April 5, 1986, Mom's water broke after she had just sat down to a Chinese take-out dinner with Dad and my maternal grandmother (affectionately called Nana), who was visiting from Buffalo. My grandfather (Papa) had flown back to Buffalo earlier that day

1

because he had to return to work as an elementary school principal.

Evidently, I've liked Chinese food since before I was born; I wanted to enter the world and try some of my own!

Dad drove Mom and Nana to Holmes Regional Medical Center (HRMC) and checked in just after midnight. Catholics and other Christians believe Sunday should be a day of rest. Alas, the Sunday I was born was a day not of rest but of labor for Mom.

According to my birth certificate, I was born at 9:38 A.M. on April 6. My head was so large due to hydrocephalus (water on the brain) that the crowning process lasted longer than it should have (there, I said it; I have a big head). While Mom labored through the night, Dad and Nana kept her company. Nana told me she got excited when she saw my head appear and then disappear in the crowning process. Subsequently, the doctor performed an episiotomy and used forceps to deliver me.

My parents jokingly considered naming me Halley after Halley's Comet, which was visible in the night sky shortly before I was born. After considering several names, they decided to name me Ashley Marie McGrath. Ashley was the second most popular baby girl's name in 1986 according to the Social Security Administration. My parents' main reason for choosing my full name is when some of its letters are rearranged, they spell out my grandmothers' names, Margaret and Shirley. My name and date of birth were added to the Cradle Roll (a wall of fame display) on the third floor at the hospital.

Certain problems were evident immediately, and doctors were consulted for their advice. My birth records contain a note from a prominent local plastic surgeon named Dr. Roxanne Guy (who has made guest appearances on *The Oprah Winfrey Show* [1986-2011] and other talk shows). Dr. Guy wrote my prognosis and advice on how to handle my special needs. This wasn't the last time she would see me, for we reunited five years later when she performed a life-changing surgery on me.

I was unable to breastfeed or drink from a bottle due to my soft cleft palate (a hole in the roof of my mouth), and a tube was inserted into my nose for nourishment. I had to stay in the hospital until I could consume the milk from a bottle within two hours by being force-fed, which Mom and Dad made sure I could do a day after Mom was released from the hospital. Before I could go home, my parents also had to take an infant CPR course.

Because of my hypotonia (low muscle tone) and tracheomalacia (weak and narrow respiratory tract), I was sent home with a heart monitor, which I used every night for eleven months. The only time the monitor alarm went off was when I had the hiccups. For eight months during my first year, a respite care nurse occasionally came to my house to take my vitals and care for me while my parents went out for a couple of hours. Mom and Dad were advised not to let me cry for fear of my throat closing up. This was probably one of their biggest challenges during my first year, especially during car trips. I was used to being held, so I didn't like sitting in my baby car seat.

Diagnosis and Prognosis

Within my first three months, I was diagnosed with *campomelic syndrome* (also known as *campomelic dysplasia*) by a genetic specialist near Orlando, Florida. The doctor arrived at this conclusion from his observations and my blood test results. Based on the high mortality rates of children with my genetic disorder due to breathing difficulties, my prognosis wasn't good.

Mom told me the geneticist gave an ominous warning to her and Dad: "Ashley might not live to see her first birthday; if she does, she may be mentally challenged. My advice to you is take her home and just love her."

Thankfully, my parents took my doctor's advice to heart and have always loved me unconditionally.

Relatives' First Visits

I've also felt the love from my extended family. Relatives such as my Aunt Kelly (Mom's younger sister who was pregnant with her own daughter at the time) traveled over a thousand miles to visit me during my first year of life. In addition, my paternal grandparents, Margaret (Peg) and Martin McGrath, visited shortly after my birth. Grandpa, whose hobby is photography, took several pictures of me during his visit. When asked what they thought when they saw me for the first time, Grandma and Grandpa said, "We thought you were the most beautiful baby on Earth. You looked like a bundle from heaven."

Grandma and Grandpa have lived in Dad's childhood home in West Seneca, New York, since 1957. Grandpa was a meat cutter for western New York grocery store chains. A few years after her youngest of six children started kindergarten, Grandma (who had different jobs early on) worked as a hospital billing clerk until retirement. As stated in a newspaper article, she said I (with my restrictive lung capacity) was one of the reasons she decided to quit smoking. Although my paternal grandparents have lived 1,200 miles north of me my whole life, I feel close to them and enjoy staying at their house every year.

Two of my uncles (Dad's younger brothers) from up north, Jim and Gerry, visited my parents and me right after my first Christmas. By that time, I had two cousins, Ben and Katie, so my family grew quite a bit in 1986. I'm grateful for the relationships I've maintained with my extended family since my first year.

First Visits to Western New York

I was the first grandchild of my four grandparents. Two of them are also my godparents, which makes their role in my life extra special. My baptism was attended by many relatives, and it was a joyous occasion. During the papacy of Pope John Paul II, I was baptized by the late Monsignor Richard Crumlish on Sunday, July 27, 1986, at St. Bonaventure's Roman Catholic Church near Grandma and Grandpa's house. This was the church where all seven of my paternal cousins were later baptized. Although the church building still stands, St. Bonaventure's was consolidated into another parish after the year 2000. One of my grandparents' neighbors painted and gave me a picture of the church to remember it.

Not long after my baptism, my hydrocephalus miraculously disappeared, and I was able to drink from a bottle on my own.

Coincidence? I think not.

Two months after my baptism, my great-grandfather James J. McGrath (the last of my father's grandparents) passed away. My parents and I flew back to Buffalo for his funeral. I wish I had the opportunity to know Great-Grandpa McGrath, an immigrant from Ireland. I would've asked him about life in his native country and his journey to the United States. Thankfully, I have memories of my maternal great-grandparents, Joseph and Beatrice Jensen, who were present at Christmas gatherings. Joseph died in 1994 followed by Beatrice six years later. I have photographs of them, including one from 1988 of the three of us on my parents' couch in Florida.

4

My First Year: I'm Still Here

On the day after my first Thanksgiving, Mom took me to my pediatrician because of my loud, barking cough. I was admitted into Holmes Regional with croup. Due to my fragile condition, I spent my first Christmas in sunny Florida instead of snowy New York as originally planned. My parents and I had Christmas dinner with neighbors who had three children, two boys under the age of five and a baby girl who happened to be born in the same hospital on the same day as I.

Years later, I had play dates with one of the girl's brothers, Aaron, who was the closest thing to a boyfriend I've ever had. The family has moved away since then, but we still keep in touch.

I beat the odds to see my first birthday in April of 1987. We had a quiet celebration at home, and my parents were overjoyed to see me make it this far. A professional photographer took a picture of me sitting in a small rocking chair that once belonged to Papa as a child. Immediately after the photo was snapped, I slid off the rocker, making a soft landing on my afghan. I still possess this family heirloom.

I was making progress in physical therapy, and despite my medical issues, I was relatively healthy. However, due to the challenges of my first year, uncertainty about my future, and the 25% probability of *campomelic syndrome* appearing in additional children, my parents decided I would be an only child. Now, all they could do was wait and see what would become of their baby girl.

Chapter 2

Pushing Through Preschool

"Although there are still occasional obstacles, the ADA
has given me greater opportunities to live an active life."

After my first birthday, my parents enrolled me in preschool. This helped me develop social skills by interacting with other kids while giving Mom a little time for herself three days a week.

At the Bottom of the ARC

I have vague memories of going to preschool at the ARC Center in Melbourne, but Mom remembers the time a little girl bit me in the face. The story goes like this: I was just minding my own business when all of a sudden, this girl, who was being weaned off her pacifier, came my way. My cheek apparently resembled her pacifier, so she sank her teeth into my face. Fortunately, one of the teachers quickly separated us. There was no blood, and the teeth marks eventually faded.

A few days later, my teacher told Mom when the same girl came within a foot of me, I (not being able to talk) stuck out my hand towards her as if to say, "Stop!" So, I had learned how to defend myself. Who knew preschool could be so dangerous? I'm glad I don't remember this incident.

Of course, there were many good days at preschool, including my third birthday, which I celebrated with my fellow preschoolers, teachers, Mom, Grandma, and Grandpa. Grandpa and I had fun when he spun me around on a red Sit 'n' Spin.™

Taking My Wheels to Creel

After two years at the ARC Center, I transferred to W. J. Creel Elementary School in Melbourne for voluntary pre-kindergarten (VPK). This was a significant milestone for me because it was the first time I rode on a school bus; it was a sixteen-mile trip one-way. I had mostly good days at Creel, but there were a few less favorable ones. One time after getting out of the school swimming pool, my ankle-foot orthotic (AFO) braces were put on the wrong feet. Not able to talk, I tried to indicate to the teacher's aide what she was doing by shaking my head, but she thought I was being uncooperative. I wore the braces on the wrong feet for hours until I finally got off the bus at home. Mom could tell by the look on my face how uncomfortable I was. To express her frustration, she called my teacher, who apologized for my distress. To make sure this incident never happened again, Mom labeled my braces "L" for left and "R" for right.

One of my best days at Creel happened during the Christmas season of 1989. "Santa Claus" visited my school and gave gifts to the preschoolers. I received a Lite Brite™ set, which turned out to be one of my favorite childhood toys. I spent numerous hours inserting multi-colored pegs into black paper templates to make beautiful images. This activity improved my fine motor skills and planted the seed for my interest in the arts.

When I wasn't at preschool, one of my favorite places to go with Mom was the mall. There were several things I enjoyed doing at the mall. I would ride on a horse in the miniature carousel, throw pennies in the fountain, browse in the dollar store, and eat chocolate chip cookies sold by a cookie vendor. I liked having a routine, so if Mom forgot to do one of these activities with me, I let her know about it! Once I started elementary school, our trips to the mall were much less frequent.

One of my favorite pastimes is reading. I attribute this partly to Dad, who read to me at least one bedtime story every night while I was in preschool. This prepared me well for when I learned to read at school. Today, I make an effort to set aside time every day to read.

Learning Sign Language

I spoke nothing but gibberish by the time I was in preschool. Some people may have misinterpreted my gibberish as a sign of a mental handicap, but my parents were convinced my soft cleft palate was the cause. Because I lacked verbal communications skills, I received speech therapy at Creel Elementary. Outside of school, I saw another speech pathologist, who taught me American Sign Language (ASL) as an alternative form of communication, in addition to a picture board I used at school. She sent me home with an introductory ASL video, and it didn't take me long to learn the basics.

A few days after I watched the ASL video, Mom placed her sewing kit on the floor by me. Multiple spools of thread were spread out as she was getting ready to sew a button on a shirt. Mom noticed me making hand gestures. After a while, she recognized my gestures were actually signs of the color of each thread she picked up. Emotion overcame Mom as she realized my ability to learn.

Before being introduced to ASL, I could only communicate with my parents through sounds and pointing, which sometimes made it difficult for them to figure out what I wanted. ASL made it less complicated and less frustrating for me to communicate until I was able to begin speaking a few years later. Mom and I still communicate through ASL occasionally when we're not sitting together or at places where we have to be quiet.

Christmas with the McGraths and the Jensens

My earliest Christmas memories are from when I was a preschooler. Throughout my life, I've spent less than a handful of Christmases in Florida. Starting as a baby in 1987, I have celebrated my favorite holiday most years with my extended family in western New York, where I saw snow for the first time. Before joining other relatives up north, my parents and I had a pre-Christmas celebration with Nana and Papa in Florida to give us an opportunity to spend quality time together during the busy holiday season.

Since the trip was costly (whether by car or plane), my parents considered being with their extended families for the holidays their gift to each other. However, they always gave me presents and a stocking full of goodies for Christmas. During our stay, we would spend Christmas Eve with Dad's family and Christmas Day with Mom's family. This way, we were able to spend the holidays with both families. Additionally, my parents and I went to church to remember the reason for the season. We also had the opportunity to celebrate the birthday of my cousin Natalie (Uncle Gerry's younger daughter) on December 27.

Knowing some people don't see their extended families for years, I feel fortunate to have been able to spend many Christmases in western New York. I hope to continue this tradition for as long as my parents and I are able to.

Being Mistaken for a Doll

Throughout my life, young children have reacted to me in different and sometimes comical ways. I have a cousin named Katie (Aunt Kelly's oldest daughter) who is seven months younger than I am. One day when

Katie was two years old, she noticed me lying down on the floor and not moving very much.

She asked my mom, "Aunt Tracy, can I play with your dolly?"

"That's not a dolly, Katie," said Mom. "That's your cousin Ashley."

"OK," said Katie, pausing. "Aunt Tracy, can I play with your dolly?"

"Ashley's not a dolly," said Mom calmly, "but yes, you can play with her. Just be careful, please."

Thankfully, Katie played with me gently that time. I have a video from the following year during which Katie is seen playfully pushing me, causing me to tip over on the floor. After a while, she realized I was a living, breathing girl like her.

A Few Accidents

One day when I was a preschooler, I was sitting in my peach-colored wheelchair in the front passenger seat of Mom's light blue Chevy Monte Carlo™ while Mom drove. All of a sudden, I felt a bump behind me, and my chair tipped over slightly to the left. I didn't get hurt, but I wondered at the time what had happened. Mom told me years later a car had bumped into the back of her car that day. The accident caused some damage to Mom's car, so my parents decided to upgrade to our first minivan, a gray Plymouth Voyager™. The minivan turned out to be a good fit for our family because it contained more space for my wheelchair and other medical equipment.

Once when Dad was off from work on a weekend, I as a preschooler woke up in the morning and crawled or rolled from my mattress on the floor to the other side of the house where my parents slept. Mom and Dad heard me giggling when I reached their room. This was the most mobile I'd ever been.

One day when I was three, I was playing on the bed in the guest room where Mom had placed me. I had gained considerable strength since being a toddler, and I was so full of energy I was rolling around. With all of my movement, I rolled off the guest bed onto the carpeted floor. My head hurt and tingled from hitting the floor. Luckily, I didn't suffer a head injury, but Mom learned a lesson: From that time on, I laid down on a blanket where I was free to roam.

As a child, I was in the habit of eating my meals lying down. While having dinner one night during my preschool years, I choked on a piece of a hot dog. Mom noticed my eyes grew wide and my lips were turning blue. So, she performed the Heimlich maneuver and succeeded in dislodging the piece of hot dog from my throat. Mom finally got to apply the skills she had learned in a CPR class. After that, she cut my meat into smaller pieces to prevent this from happening again. Nowadays, I eat my meals while sitting.

Not too long after my choking scare, Mom and I went to a restaurant for breakfast after a doctor's appointment. Before we left the parking lot, I wanted to be a big girl and help Mom open our van door. I accidentally got my left hand stuck in the door handle and panicked. Fortunately, there were a couple of firemen with their truck nearby, so Mom flagged them down. The men saw what happened and discussed what to do.

"I think we have to cut this off," said one of the firemen.

"My daughter's finger?!" asked Mom.

"No, the door handle," said the fireman.

Within two minutes, the firemen removed the door handle, and my fingers were purple and flattened. Fortunately, we had a cooler with ice from our doctor's appointment. Mom put my hand in the ice, and my fingers looked normal in no time.

I'm convinced my guardian angel was with me during these accidents, and I gave her a workout.

Nana and Papa's Move to Florida

In western New York, my maternal grandfather Robert "Bob" Jensen was a teacher and then a principal while my grandmother Shirley was a homemaker and babysitter. Papa retired from the school system in 1987. Within a year, my grandparents, my Uncle Bobby, and their black cat Heather temporarily moved in with us while they began to look for a Florida home. During this period, Papa and I were hospitalized at the same time at Holmes Regional. Papa underwent surgery for a new pacemaker and was recovering in the cardiac unit. Meanwhile, I was in the pediatric intensive care unit with bronchitis, croup, and a bleeding stress ulcer. I was forced to rest in a tented crib emitting vapors that Mom wasn't allowed to enter. At almost age two, I was mad at Mom for not cuddling with me, which elevated my heart rate. My pediatrician then told Mom it would be best if she didn't visit me as often. So, Mom was able to focus more on Papa because during that time, Nana was in western New York helping Aunt Kelly with her newborn twins, Lindsey and Donny.

Papa and I recovered in a timely manner, and despite this setback,

Nana and Papa proceeded to rent a mobile home for a year in Barefoot Bay, a community about fifteen miles south of Palm Bay. They ultimately decided to buy a home of their own there to enjoy the Florida lifestyle. It was a joy to have them living close by. We spent countless days together over the years, and Nana and Papa often babysat me while my parents played volleyball or had a date night.

Respite Care with Rikki

Because of my challenges, I couldn't just have the neighborhood teen babysitter. For additional childcare options, my parents were referred to a trained caregiver through a local respite care program. At least twice a month, I went to my respite caregiver Rikki's house for a couple of hours. Rikki's teenage son Scott played video games and introduced me to Nintendo™. There was no looking back! Playing video games actually turned out to be beneficial for me because it improved my hand-eye coordination and hand dexterity.

Mom and Dad sold their upright player piano when I was six so they could buy me a Nintendo™ system of my own. Scott generously gave me one of his video games we played together. Today, I still enjoy playing on my Nintendo Wii™.

One night with Rikki, I became ill and vomited. I was having trouble breathing, so she called 911 and my parents. I was taken away for the first time in an ambulance to Holmes Regional. After chest X-rays and hours in the ER, it turned out that I had a minor stomach virus. In spite of this unpleasant experience, I will always have fond memories of Rikki and her family. When I was in high school, I had the pleasure of attending and handing out programs at Scott's wedding. We still keep in touch today.

Mom's Attempts at Rediscovery

Even though Dad's work kept our family financially stable, Mom decided to take on part-time jobs when I was a preschooler. Along with class credits toward her Bachelor degree, she had a degree formerly known as an Associate in Secretarial Science (which she proudly refers to as her ASS). Mom worked as a consultant for Discovery Toys™, an educational company for children with and without disabilities. She hosted home parties where she sold toys and books. After six months, she earned the option of purchasing items for me at a discounted rate.

I benefitted from numerous hours playing with toys such as stacking cups, chain rings, and a structure of tubes with rolling marbles.

Other times, Mom entertained children at birthday parties by dressing as a clown like Bozo. Having watched Bozo every week on TV, I was spellbound when I saw him perform onstage at the Melbourne Auditorium in 1988.

For the second birthday of my twin cousins Lindsey and Donny who were visiting Nana and Papa, Mom wore her clown costume, a yellow outfit with green buttons, white face paint, a red nose, and a red curly wig. I almost didn't recognize my own mother. We all enjoyed this fun side of her.

After trying these odd jobs for a year, Mom decided to focus on being a stay-at-home mother.

Family Connection to the Gulf War

Even though I was too young to be interested in politics, world events touched my life. While the period known as the Cold War was coming to an end, my Aunt Kathie's husband Mike, a mechanic by trade, fought in the Gulf War in 1990 as a member of the Coast Guard Reserves. In the meantime, Aunt Kathie and their two little boys Ben and Nick tried to live their lives as usual in their home near Buffalo. During this time, Mom and I stayed at their house for a week. I received a photograph in the mail from Uncle Mike on his ship. I thought he was so brave and looked up to him as a hero.

Aunt Kathie missed Uncle Mike very much, but she was a strong military wife. I remember how excited I was to see Uncle Mike again the next time I went to Buffalo. My excitement didn't compare to the joy Aunt Kathie and her sons felt upon Uncle Mike's safe return. Within a couple of years, their youngest son Ryan, my parents' godson, was born. Uncle Mike was deployed once more in 2003 and returned home safely again where he continued his work as a mechanic until his retirement last year.

ADA's Impact on My Life

While Uncle Mike fought in the Gulf War, I continued to fight my "war" against my disabilities. I was four years old when President George H. W. Bush signed the Americans with Disabilities Act (ADA) into law on July 26, 1990. I wasn't aware at that time of the significance of that historic day, but looking back now, I know the ADA contributed to my ability to receive a good education with accommodations to meet my special needs.

Additionally, the ADA made people with disabilities like me feel more respected and important than ever before. The new law made local and long-distance travel easier for my parents and me by giving us the option to park in handicapped spots near the front doors of establishments, move up ramps instead of stairs, and use elevators in multi-story buildings. Pre-boarding airplanes and cruise ships shortens waiting times. Staying in handicapped accessible hotel rooms gives me more room for my wheelchair. Handicapped seating and assistive listening devices make going to the movies more enjoyable.

Although there are still occasional obstacles such as illegal parking in handicapped spots by the nondisabled and malfunctioning elevators, the ADA has given me greater opportunities to live an active life.

First Surgeries

During my second year of life, my ear, nose, and throat (ENT) specialist told my parents I needed T-tubes implanted into my ears to reduce ear infections and maintain hearing in my right ear. I had no hearing at all in my left ear, so this operation was important to preserve the hearing I had left. On August 31, 1988, I underwent my first surgery at a same-day surgery center near Holmes Regional.

The procedure took longer than expected because of breathing complications, requiring close monitoring by a pediatric anesthesiologist, who also provided anesthesia during several other surgeries of mine. The operation was successful, the ear infections less frequent, and there has been no additional hearing loss. My ENT specialist gave my green ear tubes to my parents, who put them in my baby album. In recent years, my doctor has referred to me as a "waxy lady" because he's had to clean my ears every three to four months.

Two years later, my parents noticed I wasn't crawling, kneeling, or sitting myself up as I previously had. Following visits to my orthopedic surgeon and my neurosurgeon, myelogram test results showed I had spinal stenosis, a narrowing of the spine which presses on the spinal cord. I needed a major back operation to correct it.

On June 5, 1991, my orthopedic surgeon and my neurosurgeon performed a posterior laminectomy to remove part of a bone in my spine at Arnold Palmer Hospital for Children and Women in Orlando. The surgery stabilized my back to prevent further weakness in my legs, and my legs improved, regaining some strength for a while.

Age Five and Still Alive

One of my fondest memories from early childhood is my fifth birthday party held at Friendly's Restaurant in April of 1991. I was excited because this was my first real party. My parents, Nana, and Papa were there along with many of my preschool classmates and their parents. Everybody sang the birthday song before I blew out the candles on the cake. One gift I received was my first video, which contained an episode of *Mister Rogers' Neighborhood* (1968-2001), one of my favorite TV shows at that time.

By age five, I had already exceeded my doctors' expectations for children with *campomelic syndrome*. The medical issues I had were manageable. I was ready for the next chapter of my life.

Chapter 3

Unlocking My Potential at Lockmar

"Coping with my friend's passing made me realize for the first time how precious life is."

After completing preschool and recovering from back surgery, my parents registered me to begin kindergarten at Creel Elementary. Right before the start of the 1991-1992 school year, my parents decided to move me to Lockmar Elementary, which also had an excellent program for students with special needs and was only three miles from home.

Kindergarten and First Grade

When Mom called Lockmar to inquire about enrollment, she got in touch with Devorah Hollinger, a welcoming guidance counselor who led Mom through the process of enrolling. Throughout my elementary school years, Mrs. Hollinger, who happened to live less than a mile from us, was an invaluable resource. She came to my house to tutor me a few times while I was recovering from various surgeries even though she was battling cancer, which she survived. Mrs. Hollinger went above and beyond her call of duty as a guidance counselor, and I'll always be thankful for her help.

I started at Lockmar during the second week of the semester. Back on the school bus I went, sporting my new pink back brace. Since I had gone to daycare and preschool, kindergarten wasn't too scary for me. My kindergarten teacher (whom I recently saw at my church after twenty years) had a teacher's aide familiar with sign language. All of my five classmates had different special needs, also known at our school as "varying exceptionalities." I stood out by being the only student in my class in a wheelchair.

One of my best memories of kindergarten was playing Goldilocks in my class's version of "Goldilocks and the Three Bears." My parents still have a video of my class play. I appeared to be quite the aspiring actress.

Seriously, my biggest challenge in kindergarten was learning how to write. I recall just scribbling and doodling on my journal pages because I didn't know what to write. Thankfully, my writing improved by the time I entered the first grade. In addition to my daily classes were weekly sessions of art, computer, music, and reading time in the school library. I also received physical, occupational, and speech therapies and met with a hearing itinerant every week.

For a couple of weeks, I went outside for recess with my kindergarten classmates, but one day, I became dehydrated in the late summer heat. Mom took me to the pediatrician, and I recovered quickly at home. After returning to school, I was forced to stay inside with students in detention during recess until cooler weather came. This was no fun, but I didn't have any other option.

In October of 1991, my classmates went on a field trip to a petting zoo and a pumpkin patch. Mom decided not to take me to the zoo at that time because she felt it was too hot outside for me. So that I wouldn't miss out on my classmates' experience, she took me to the petting zoo when it was cooler. I fed a goat, which showed its appreciation by chomping down on my left index finger. Fortunately, I was able to take my finger out of the goat's mouth before its teeth broke through my skin, but it took a while for me to get near an animal again.

Before I completed kindergarten, I underwent two life-changing surgeries, which I describe later.

In the first grade, my class once again had other kids with disabilities (mostly wheelchair users). I'll never forget my teacher, Betty Bishop, who passed away when I was in high school.

First grade is the year I learned how to tell time. I struggled with this concept at school, so my parents gave me a book about time and tutored me during one weekend. By Monday morning at 8:00, I was able to tell time. My parents and I were proud I achieved this goal in a "timely" manner.

On my seventh birthday, which was much better than my sixth birthday spent in the hospital, I enjoyed watching a softball game in which my babysitter Rikki's son Scott played. Scott was like a big brother to me at that time, so I enjoyed being around him.

Finding My Voice

While I was in preschool, I watched an animated series called *Maya the Bee* (1990-1992). Grandpa took an audio recording of me attempting to sing the show's theme song. Although I couldn't enunciate well due to my soft cleft palate, my family knew I had the potential to talk.

Since my previous operations went well, my parents decided it was time for my soft cleft palate to be repaired. We had a consultation with my plastic surgeon Dr. Roxanne Guy, and she agreed to perform the surgery.

Five days before Christmas of 1991, Dr. Guy operated on me at Holmes Regional. Two weeks later, gauze (which resembled to me a long, green vegetable like spinach) was removed from the roof of my mouth while Dr. Guy's husband took photos for my records. I was shocked at that time to see how much gauze was packed in my mouth. According to Dr. Guy, the first words that came out of my mouth were, "Hi, Dr. Guy!"

My new-found ability to speak made life much easier for my parents and me. It also led to a funny and memorable conversation I had with Papa at Friendly's when I was about seven years old. I didn't eat very much when I was a child because I felt full quickly. On this day at Friendly's with my family, I ate about one-half of my hot dog and a few French fries before declaring I was full.

Papa responded, "Ashley, may I please have the rest of your hot dog?"

"Didn't you already have your lunch?" I said.

"Yes, I did," said Papa, "but I have enough room for your hot dog."

"You're not too full?" I asked.

"No, honey," said Papa.

"Well, you *look* full," I said.

My comment made Papa laugh so hard, and he told many people about my tactful comment over the years. At the time I said those words, I was politely referring to his girth, but I've come to realize Papa was truly full—full of humor, wisdom, and, most of all, love.

Sweatin' with Richard

I wasn't overweight as a child, but exercising was not easy due to my limited mobility. By this time in my life, I'd had a couple of major back surgeries which took weeks to months of recovery. I needed a way to stay fit in addition to the physical therapy at school.

One day when I was six, Mom found an exercise video for the physically challenged by Richard Simmons called *Reach for Fitness* (1986). Not only did the video present exercises that could be done sitting on a chair, it also showed children exercising while lying down on exercise mats. After briefly talking about eating healthy foods, Richard began the exercise segment by encouraging everybody to say, "I can do it!"

I enjoyed moving to the music and following Richard's instructions delivered in an enthusiastic manner. This became a fun supplement to physical therapy.

On March 27, 1993, Richard made an appearance at the Melbourne Square Mall near my house. Mom, Nana, and I went to the mall to watch the exercise show, where I noticed another child in a wheelchair from my school with his mom. After the show, we waited over an hour in line to meet Richard. Unlike Mom and Nana, I was very patient, and I didn't care how long I'd have to wait; I was so excited because Richard Simmons would be the first celebrity I had ever met.

When it was finally my turn, I gave Richard a letter Mom helped me write to let him know the impact his video had on my life. He gave me an autographed photo and a kiss on the cheek. This was one of the most exciting moments of my first seven years of life.

Sometimes, I still exercise to *Reach for Fitness*, and whenever I see him in the media, it reminds me of the day I sweated with Richard Simmons at the mall.

In addition to exercising with my Richard Simmons video, I attempted to strengthen my legs during cooler months by riding a low-rider tricycle, which I eventually donated to a special needs organization. Dad accompanied me on my tricycle trips. The favorite part of my ride was when I let my tricycle go down my parents' driveway without pedaling because it made me feel like I was going fast.

Now, I use a handcycle to transport myself around the neighborhood. The handcycle attaches to the front of my manual wheelchair. Turning the handles in a circular motion with my hands propels me forward. While strengthening my upper body muscles and working up a sweat, I get to enjoy nature.

My Days with Dad

My cousin Tess, my Aunt Bonnie's daughter, was born on September 14, 1993. Later in the month, Mom flew to Buffalo for a long weekend to visit her newborn niece among other relatives. Meanwhile back in Florida, Dad and I were left to fend for ourselves for three days, the longest time in my life Mom and I were apart. Since Mom was my primary caretaker, this weekend was different for Dad and me. I knew I was in good hands because my dad is one of the gentlest men I know. However, I was concerned at age seven my daily routine would be altered because Dad didn't do things quite like Mom did.

One night, I wanted chocolate milk, my favorite beverage. Instead of just asking Dad for the chocolate milk, I wanted to make it myself, in an effort to be independent. After grabbing a cup and a spoon, I opened the refrigerator door to get chocolate syrup. Then, I looked at the gallon of milk, which was too heavy for me to lift and pour without making a mess. Next to the milk, I saw a carton of Half and Half™ creamer. The creamer resembled milk to me, so I thought it was a good substitute. After mixing everything together, I took a sip and noticed my "chocolate milk" was thicker than usual. I realized then Half and Half™ was not the same as milk, and I never tried to make chocolate milk by myself ever again.

Dad, who actually made a fine "Mr. Mom," and I had a fun time and bonded together the weekend Mom was gone. We played Nintendo™, ate at McDonald's™, and went to church, among other activities. Before we knew it, Mom was home again. Telling me how much she missed me, Mom admitted she cried during the flight to Buffalo. I was glad to see Mom again, but this experience taught me a little time without her wasn't such a bad thing.

Second and Third Grades

Before I entered second grade, my guidance counselor informed my parents of the possibility for me to be mainstreamed, which meant I'd be placed in a class with non-disabled students. To determine if this was a viable option for me, I spent part of the school day in a regular first grade classroom for several days. With assistance, I was able to keep up with the other students.

The next step was an oral exam, which I passed. My guidance counselor then assisted my parents in making necessary changes to my Individualized Education Program (IEP), detailing the accommodations I needed as a student with disabilities.

Being mainstreamed was a turning point for me academically. I was accustomed to a class of five to ten students. Now, my class had twenty-five children, but I got along well with my classmates. I realized during this year how popular my name was, for there was at least one other Ashley in my class. Therefore, I was referred to as "Ashley M." for the rest of my elementary school years to distinguish myself from the other Ashleys.

My second grade teacher, Mrs. Harris, made my transition into mainstreamed education as smooth as it could be. The class work was more difficult, but I did well enough. The classroom was equipped with speakers that amplified Mrs. Harris's voice into my hearing aid. A teacher's aide, Mrs. Seekamp, was like another mother to me.

I can understand why Mrs. Seekamp signed my sixth grade yearbook as my "second mom" because she was very helpful to me at elementary school. She gave me her full attention while my teacher was busy with my classmates. Mrs. Harris has moved out of state while Mrs. Seekamp stayed in the area.

Shortly after starting second grade, I went with my parents to a gathering of children with *campomelic syndrome* and their families in Great Falls, Montana, over Labor Day weekend in 1993. Mom's thirty-sixth birthday took place around that time, which I happily announced during a video recorded that weekend by singing, "Mommy's aging, Mommy's aging!"

While in Montana, we had the pleasure of meeting Dr. John Opitz, one of the genetic researchers who named this disorder, years before I was born. My parents and I went on a brief boat ride on the Missouri River, the same river on which explorers Lewis and Clark traveled on their way to the Pacific Ocean. I saw mountain goats and bald eagles along the way. An article about our gathering was published in *The Great Falls Tribune*, and I brought it to school for Show and Tell.

One of my favorite memories from second grade was being the "star" of the school play "Mrs. Sun." I was dressed in yellow and wore a spiky headband that represented sun rays. I was positioned in the middle of the stage, pretending to sew a quilt with "Mrs. Cloud" (who happened to be one of my first grade classmates also in a wheelchair) while the other characters sang and danced around us. I can still hear the theme song we sang, which contained the following lyrics: "Mrs. Sun, Sun, Mrs. Golden Sun, please shine down on me!"

Another fun memory I have from second grade is playing with a stuffed Paddington Bear, which every student would take turns keeping for a week. We took pictures of Paddington wherever we went and wrote brief entries in a journal about what we did during our week together. It was hard for me to give Paddington Bear back at the end of my week with him, but it was a unique assignment that taught my classmates and me how to document events that took place in our lives.

As a second grader, I also felt a little more grown-up because my parents started giving me a weekly allowance of four dollars for behaving well, getting good grades, and doing a chore such as folding laundry. This taught me responsibility and the value of a dollar. I don't remember the things I bought with my allowance back then, but I do remember how good it felt to be rewarded for my hard work.

During the week of my eighth birthday, I had a party with my female classmates at home. First, we gathered in the sun porch where we had refreshments and cake. Then, my friends and I went to the garage where we swung at a piñata in an effort to break it open for the candy to drop out. I didn't have the strength to break a piñata apart, but I enjoyed trying because it was a tradition at the annual McGrath family picnic near Buffalo. My birthday party gave me the opportunity to interact with my classmates outside of school and have fun like any kid.

Since my previous birthday party was so much fun, I had another party for my ninth birthday with my classmates at home, this time without a piñata. During third grade, my school work showed signs of improvement, thanks in part to my teacher, Mrs. Red, whose surname also happens to be my favorite color.

Mom was the "room mom," so she hosted holiday parties for my class throughout the year. At the Halloween class party, Mom brought a mystery guest who wore a costume that made the guest unrecognizable. After my classmates and I spent a few minutes guessing the mystery guest's identity, she revealed herself as the school library aide. Knowing how to throw a fun party, Mom was very involved at my school; she was also an Apple Corp volunteer and a Math Superstars teacher for gifted students (which she admitted was ironic because she wasn't great at math, but she made do with an answer key).

In May of 1995, I received the Catholic sacrament of First Communion. I had prepared for this event by attending weekly religious education classes. I knew I needed help moving toward the priest when it was my turn to receive communion, but I didn't want one of my parents to push me in my wheelchair.

At age nine, I felt self-conscious about depending on my parents' assistance all the time. In an effort to appear more independent, I asked my religious education teacher to push my wheelchair, and she agreed. This way, my parents were able to proudly witness my First Communion from their seats like the other parents.

Dressed in white similar to the day of my Baptism, this time with a veil, I received my first host (wafer) and took my first sip of wine, which tasted to me like medicine at the time. This moment made me feel like a more active participant in my religion.

I also participated in the sacrament of First Penance and Reconciliation in which I confessed my misdeeds to a priest. Although I like to think I was a relatively well-behaved child, I had my moments of rebellion. Going through my first confession made me realize I was accountable not only to my parents, but also to my priest and ultimately to God. This made me consider my behavior more carefully and instilled in me a sense of maturity.

I have a confession to make: Since one of my nicknames is Ash, I thought as a child that Ash Wednesday, the first day of Lent, was a day about me, like a birthday. Isn't it funny how kids think sometimes? After a while, I realized it's not always about me; it's about Him.

Fourth and Fifth Grades

My fourth grade teacher was Mrs. Louzon, who goes to my church. Mrs. Louzon, who had a teacher intern for part of the school year, started each morning by playing music to which my classmates and I danced. My favorite song back then was C+C Music Factory's "Gonna Make You Sweat," which made me bounce in my wheelchair upon hearing these famous opening lyrics: "Everybody dance now!" This activity allowed my classmates and me to have a little fun and expend a little extra energy before we focused on learning.

My classmates and I sometimes sang a song about state capitals, and Mrs. Louzon posted the lyrics on a projector. One day, we were singing when I realized one of the state capitals was missing from the list: Juneau, Alaska. After the song was over, I raised my hand and pointed out the omission to Mrs. Louzon. Surprised by what I said, she played the song over again and realized I was right.

"Good job, Ashley," said Mrs. Louzon. "I've been using this list for over ten years, and you're the first to notice Juneau was missing."

Mrs. Louzon is from North Carolina, so she has a distinctive Southern accent. By the end of every school week, I found myself talking like her. Perhaps I enjoyed having Mrs. Louzon for a teacher so much I wanted to emulate her, but my adoption of her accent probably happened because her voice was amplified in my ear by my hearing aid for hours every day. During the weekend, my normal voice returned, only to be replaced by Mrs. Louzon's drawl again on Monday. This amused my family.

My fourth grade classmates and I went on a field trip to SeaWorld in Orlando. I was fascinated by the whales, seals, and dolphins among other animals in their massive glass tanks. While I was in the hospital recovering from back surgery later in the school year, Mrs. Louzon sent me a stuffed dolphin that made a noise when it was squeezed.

For Thanksgiving in 1995, my parents and I stayed at a resort. Dad and I swam in the pool with a boy who had been recovering from chickenpox. Within a couple of weeks, there were red, itchy dots on my body. I went to my pediatrician, and sure enough, I had chickenpox. I missed a week of school. Mom gave me oatmeal baths, which soothed my skin. The most challenging part of chickenpox was resisting the urge to itch. I'm glad I can't contract chickenpox again.

In the same year, I completed my first science fair project. The project involved observing the growth of mold on dry and wet slices of bread. I hypothesized there'd be more mold on wet bread, which is exactly what happened. Since my parents didn't have a computer yet, I had to write everything on my display board by hand as neatly as I could. During speech therapy one day, I was pleasantly surprised to hear over the PA system I had won first place in my category at the school science fair. There was an article about my science fair win in the local newspaper. I didn't advance beyond the regional science fair that year, but this sparked my interest in science.

I was almost ten years old when I first grasped the concept of death. In March of 1996, a friend of mine, who also used a wheelchair and had respiratory problems, passed away. I didn't spend much time with my friend, but I was affected nonetheless when Mom gave me this news. I was stunned and frightened, for this made me aware of my own mortality.

Prior to this, I thought only "old people" like my great-grandfather Joe Jensen died. Mom and Dad went to my friend's funeral while I stayed with Nana and Papa. Despite my parents' efforts to keep me calm during this time, I started having anxiety attacks at bedtime. I was afraid to fall asleep thinking I wouldn't wake up. I went to counseling for a few months. The sessions with my therapist were helpful, and I began sleeping better at night.

Coping with my friend's passing made me realize for the first time how precious life is. This is a lesson I'd carry with me for the rest of my childhood and into adulthood.

I had my tenth birthday party at a local bowling alley with classmates. My younger cousin and my parents' godson Beau, who happened to be visiting from Buffalo, also attended. My classmates were confused about how I could bowl. Dad assembled my portable bowling ramp made of aluminum, positioned it in front of the lane, and handed me a bowling ball. Then, I pushed the ball, which went down the ramp (shaped like a slide) onto the lane to the pins.

This was when my friends exclaimed, "So, *that's* how you bowl!"

I may not have bowled too many strikes this way, but I was able to participate with my friends in a physical game. Another time, I bowled with Dad and Grandpa, and I had the highest score.

In July of 1996, Dad traveled to Ireland with his Uncle Ed. Dad's fortieth birthday took place during the trip. In the meantime, Mom and I stayed at Grandma and Grandpa's house and visited relatives in the Buffalo area. After two weeks, Dad returned bearing gifts for me: a green, white, and orange scarf with the word *Ireland* on it and a mathematical set.

The ruler, protractor, and other items in the mathematical set came in handy for me during geometry class years later. After Dad's trip, I developed an interest in my Irish heritage. I began collecting Irish-related items I display on a shelf. My collection was featured in the March 2006 issue of *Antiques and Collecting Magazine*.

Going to Ireland is on my bucket list.

In the fifth grade, the year Dad bought a computer, I was invited to join the Gifted Students Program (GSP) due to my above average performance on a standardized test the previous year. One day per week, I reported to a different classroom with other gifted kids. Our teacher Mrs. Heine's class sessions were interesting and informative.

My classmates and I wrote articles for the school newsletter and distributed copies to fellow students in the cafeteria. This increased my interest in writing. I was grateful for the opportunity to be in GSP because it made me enjoy school even more. This program challenged me academically and made me a better critical thinker.

For the other four days of the school week, my fifth grade teacher was Ms. Suthard with whom I still keep in touch. That year, I was part of another school play, "Bartholomew J. Harding and Friends." This time, I played a skunk that sang and danced during a musical number; I even wore a furry costume. After that, one of the lunch ladies gave me the nickname "Stinky." It was definitely a step down from my starring roles in previous plays, but it was still fun.

For my eleventh birthday, I hosted my first pajama party with three of my good friends from school. We ate snacks and cake and watched a movie before going to bed later than usual. It was fun to spend quality time with a few of my friends.

Outside of school, I was a member of the 4-H Club for several years. I have fond memories from this club. I caught my first fish (a blue gill) while fishing from a dock with other 4-H members. I placed first in my category at a club-sponsored public speaking competition after delivering a speech about bicycle safety. The 4-H Club was a fun outlet that improved my social skills and provided opportunities for hands-on activities.

Pitching to Papa

One of my fondest memories of Papa is watching him play in the Over-60 Softball League in Barefoot Bay. Shortly before the 1997 season opener, the league held a discussion about who should throw the first pitch. Full of grandfatherly pride, Papa "pitched" to them the idea I could be the guest opening pitcher, and the league approved. I was tickled pink when Papa told me about this opportunity, which made me feel more like a grown-up.

In November of that year, I dressed up for the part by wearing a baseball cap and Florida Marlins sunglasses and holding my baseball mitt. At the appointed time, I made my way to the pitcher's mound while Papa served as catcher. Applying my skills from Field Day at school, I threw the softball as hard as I could (which was maybe halfway between the mound and home plate), and Papa scooped it up with his glove and a smile on his face. A reporter and photographer observed the game, so I was in the newspaper once again. As a nice bonus, Papa's team won the game.

Sixth Grade

Finally, I was among the upperclassmen at school. Throughout sixth grade, I wrote in a diary almost every day to record my experiences. My homeroom/English teacher was Mrs. Balavender, whose husband also taught at Lockmar. This was the first year where I had a teacher for each subject. I had to transfer every hour to another classroom like students do in high school. This wasn't easy for me to do in a manual wheelchair, so one of my classmates helped me. This schedule helped to prepare me for the rest of my years in school.

Lockmar Elementary students were known as the Knights. It's thus appropriate a highlight of the sixth grade was a field trip to Medieval

Times near Orlando. Medieval Times is a dinner theater restaurant chain that features sword fights, jousting, and other activities performed by actors in an eleventh-century setting. My classmates and I ate chicken and potatoes without utensils, which was "finger-licking good." This experience made me feel like I traveled back in time.

Brevard County has a minor league baseball team called the Manatees, who play home games at Space Coast Stadium in Viera. On a spring night that was traditionally known as "Lockmar Night," students from the school had the opportunity to go to an evening game and sit in a certain section of the bleachers. I sat in the handicapped section with my parents, but I could see the Lockmar section from my chair. We had hot dogs, hamburgers, fries, and nacho chips for dinner. During the game, the announcer welcomed Lockmar Elementary. I don't remember if the Manatees won the game, but it was a fun night. I've gone to a few Manatees games since then.

Throughout elementary school, I had more surgeries on my spine due to scoliosis, including one during sixth grade. Before the operation in March of 1998, my teacher and classmates threw me a surprise going-away party with balloons and cake. This was one of the best days of sixth grade for me because I felt touched to have so much support going into another surgery.

A Sweet Ride

This surgery had to be done in Minneapolis. On the day we flew home after my back surgery, Mom and I waited in front of our hotel for our ride to the airport. Suddenly, a limousine entered the parking lot.

"Look, Ashley, a limousine," said Mom. "Someone famous must be here."

The limousine pulled up to where Mom and I were waiting. The chauffeur got out of the limo and approached us.

"Hello," said the chauffeur. "May I help you with your bags?"

"I think you have the wrong person," I replied.

"Ashley, he's here for us," said Mom, grinning.

I didn't expect the privilege of riding in a limousine. While Mom and I sat in the back, the chauffeur turned on the radio for us. Before I knew it, we arrived at the airport. The chauffeur didn't accept Mom's payment for the ride; he said it was "on the house." My first limousine ride made me feel extra special, especially after yet another surgery.

I continued recovering from surgery at home and was healed in time for Field Day, an annual athletic competition held at Lockmar. I competed in the ball-throwing event with other students with disabilities. I won second place, which completed my collection of Field Day ribbons: one for every ranking from first through fifth.

One of the awards I received at the end of sixth grade was a "Great Speller" award for placing third in the school spelling bee. Thinking I had to spell *conformation*, the word I misspelled was *confirmation*. I find this ironic because Confirmation is a Catholic sacrament I would receive years later. I also received an English award for performing well in that class. These awards demonstrated how much I liked to read and write.

A Not-So-Sweet Flight

Before another back surgery, my parents signed up for a free flight on a single-engine plane to Minneapolis. We took off from the northern end of Brevard County. Mom, who was nervous about flying on regular-sized airplanes, clearly didn't enjoy the small plane, which was noisy and shaky. There were also no lavatories or complimentary beverages and snacks. I enjoyed looking out the window but wished the small plane was as fast as a jet airplane.

After a layover in Tennessee, we flew on a twin-engine plane to Iowa. Then, Mom had had enough, so we stayed overnight at a hotel and traveled the rest of the way to Minneapolis in a rental car. After my surgery, we flew home non-stop on a jet. Generous people offered free flight services for children who had an upcoming operation. Although my parents and I were grateful for this service, we never took advantage of flying across the country in small planes again.

Getting Away from It All

Before I was born, my parents bought a timeshare week at Ocean Landings Resort near Ron Jon's Surf Shop in Cocoa Beach. Sitting on the balcony as a little girl, I watched and heard the sounds of the Atlantic Ocean with a sense of wonder.

My parents were able to change the timeshare's location and time of year through an exchange program. Taking advantage of this opportunity, we stayed at resorts in cities all over Florida such as Punta Gorda, Naples, and Daytona Beach. One time when we vacationed in St. Augustine (the oldest city in the United States), we visited the Fountain of Youth, toured the Ripley's Believe It or Not Museum, and saw a lighthouse.

While at another timeshare in Orlando during Thanksgiving week, Aunt Carol, my cousin George, Mom, and I saw a live show based on *American Gladiators* (1989-1996), which was one of my favorite shows at the time. During the same week, we went to Disney World to which I had been in the past. While waiting in line at the park entrance, I realized it was cool and windy, which made it hard for me to breathe when I was a kid. So, I told Mom I didn't want to go into Disney World. Being from Buffalo, George was shocked I didn't want to go to Disney World! Leaving our relatives at the "happiest place on Earth," Mom and I rented a movie and went back to our resort for a quiet and relaxing day.

Mom and Dad sold their timeshare when I was starting high school, but it was fun while it lasted.

Since many of my parents' relatives still live in western New York, I've gone there at least once every year since my birth. In a typical year, we travel during the summer and again shortly before Christmas. The summer was filled with fun: walks with Grandpa, birthday parties, fireworks, sparklers, water balloons, local carnivals, and my cousins' sporting events.

A couple of years after I was born, Dad's family began hosting a summer picnic at Chestnut Ridge Park in Orchard Park, home of the Buffalo Bills. I attended one of the Buffalo Bills' games with my parents and cousin Beau in December 2002. Beau and I had our faces painted in Bills' colors (red, white and blue) and we were glad to see the Bills win.

At the family picnic, adults engage in conversation while children participate in games such as searching for coins in a sawdust pile, breaking the piñata, a scavenger hunt, and water balloon tosses. After the games are over and the barbecue grills are fired up, the relatives have dinner together, sharing homemade dishes. My parents and I are not able to go to the McGrath picnic every year, but when we do, we treasure the time we have with Dad's ever-growing extended family.

One time, Mom and I went to a drive-in movie theater where we watched an animated version of the film *Tarzan* (1999). In addition to visiting our extended family and enjoying a different climate temporarily, my parents and I have gone to several New York attractions that sometimes supplemented my history classes.

For example, we went on a boat ride in Lockport on the Erie Canal, which I learned was the first transportation system to connect New York

City with the Great Lakes. Another summer, my parents and I visited Letchworth State Park, the site of a statue of Mary Jemison, a frontier woman who was captured and adopted as a young girl by the Seneca tribe in 1755.

A few summers after that trip, we dropped by Elmira, New York, where Mark Twain's gravesite is located. At nearby Elmira College, there is a gazebo that contains some of Twain's belongings such as his rocking chair in which I sat.

Then, we went to the National Baseball Hall of Fame in Cooperstown, which was fun yet informative. I've never gotten tired of vacationing in western New York and always look forward to my next visit.

During my childhood, I began collecting postcards as mementos of the places to which I traveled. I also asked relatives and friends to send me postcards. I have a display case full of pressed pennies from machines located at some points of interest such as zoos and museums.

The first item I collected as a child was PEZ™ dispensers. Due to lack of space, I eventually sold most of my dispensers, keeping a few of my favorites. I've enjoyed collecting because it's an activity in which I can engage regardless of my disabilities.

Chapter 4

Surgical Summaries

"I wish I didn't have to undergo intensive operations as a child, but they were necessary for the sake of my health."

I have had fifteen surgeries during my childhood. All of my doctors played an instrumental part in my well-being. Their work improved my quality of life, allowing me to pursue goals I may not have achieved otherwise. For this, I'm grateful for the doctors as well as the nurses who aided my recovery.

Shortly before Christmas in 1993, my orthopedic surgeon loosened my hamstrings and abductor muscles during a procedure at Arnold Palmer Hospital in Orlando. I was supposed to wear a spica cast that covered my legs for at least six weeks. I was relatively comfortable during the day, but the spasticity of my legs kept me up at night. For this reason, my cast was removed two weeks early and immediately replaced with a removable plastic brace. Then, I used a soft wedge when lying down to keep my legs spread apart until recovery was complete.

In 1995 my pediatric urologist removed a relatively large bladder stone, which I saw upon waking from surgery, and repaired my hernia. Mom would've kept the stone if it didn't have to be sent away for analysis. Upon the recommendation of my pediatric endocrinologist, the urologist also removed undeveloped tissue to prevent ovarian cancer later in life. Since then, I have an ultrasound done on a regular basis to monitor my smaller kidney stones.

This chapter summarizes two series of my most intensive operations, including how my parents rearranged their lives for my sake and how I recovered.

Back-to-Back Surgeries

The story of how I met my spine surgeon can be described in one word: serendipity. Aware of the urgent need for the correction of my kyphoscoliosis (curvature of the spine that results in a hunchback), my parents did research on the best doctors and surgeons in the country. In a publication mentioned on *Oprah*, Mom found a spine surgeon, who was an expert in my syndrome, in Minneapolis, Minnesota. This seemed like a far distance to travel, but an option, nonetheless. Keeping the surgeon's name in mind, my parents continued their research, and we went about our daily lives.

On the phone one day, Grandma told my parents about a friend whose grandson was seeing a surgeon in Minnesota for his scoliosis. Coincidentally, it was the same surgeon from that publication. Shortly after this, my parents received a phone call from my local orthopedic surgeon, who recommended the same surgeon.

Because of our faith, we took this as a sign from God. Mom called the surgeon's office in Minnesota and was told he was about to retire. However, the secretary invited her to schedule an appointment for us to meet with him and his colleagues in a week. Despite the short notice, Mom took the appointment and booked our flights and hotel reservations. Dad asked for time off from work and obtained authorization from his health insurance provider.

In early December of 1991, my parents and I flew to Minneapolis for a consultation with the spine surgeons, including Dr. John Lonstein, who made a commitment to operate on me. The consultation boosted my parents' confidence in this doctor, originally from South Africa.

I also saw a pulmonologist to test my lungs and trachea, which was crucial prior to this serious back surgery. In March of 1992, after a week's postponement due to my hospitalization for bronchitis, Mom and Dad took turns driving for about thirty hours in three days to Minneapolis. We couldn't fly this time because I wouldn't be able to sit upright for months after my operations. Airlines required passengers to sit during takeoff and landing.

The mother of a member of our disabilities support group generously let my parents and me stay at her apartment outside of St. Paul to save us the expense of a hotel room. During other hospital visits in Minnesota, my parents stayed at a women's shelter and at a hotel that was physically connected to the hospital, which also contained a McDonald's™. This made me happy because I had loved McDonald's™ French fries since I was a preschooler. I was so obsessed with the fries I'd beg Mom for them whenever I saw the golden arches. This led Mom to take alternate routes while driving me to avoid McDonald's™. I still enjoy having French fries on occasion.

My parents tried to explain the upcoming operation to me, but I didn't know exactly how I would look or feel after my operation. To lessen my nervousness on the day of my first surgery with Dr. Lonstein and the

Spine Surgery Center team, Dad, dressed up in scrubs with a surgical mask and head cover, came with me to the operating room and held my hand until I fell asleep. Then, an IV was inserted into my hand.

During the surgery, one surgeon deflated one of my lungs to allow access to my spine, and another surgeon broke and repaired vertebrae in my neck before fusing it. Dr. Lonstein then operated on my spine to straighten it as much as possible and prevent further curvature.

I had a respirator to help me breathe, which left me unable to speak temporarily. The surgeon inserted a chest tube and bladder catheter. Additionally, a circular metal brace called a "halo" was attached to my head with six pin sites.

I had a tendency to lose a significant amount of blood during orthopedic surgeries, so I needed blood transfusions. Fortunately, we had access to a blood bank, and my parents were able to donate directly for me.

After I regained consciousness from anesthesia in the pediatric intensive care unit (PICU), Mom gave me her makeup mirror, and I saw I had lost my first tooth, one of my two front teeth, during surgery. I was more upset about my missing tooth than being in the hospital with all of the tubes and halo!

Grandma and Uncle John, Dad's brother from Baltimore, came to visit me in the PICU. To stretch my spine slightly, I was in traction for two weeks and could be moved only when necessary. During this time, I watched television, including a hospital channel for children, and videos, read books from the hospital library, played games, and received TLC from everyone.

The worst part of the first days of recovery was when nurses would clean the inside of my respirator tube. In order to do this, they had to turn off the oxygen supply for a few seconds. Not being able to breathe for those few seconds was the most horrifying feeling in the world. After a couple of days, I was able to breathe on my own, and the respirator was removed. Pulling the tube slowly out of my nose felt strange, but it was a relief to be free of it. Regaining the ability to breathe was the first sign I was on my way to recovery, and for that, I was thankful.

Nana, who came to Minneapolis after my surgery, kept Mom and me company during most of my time in the hospital. Dad flew back and forth because he had to work and take care of household affairs.

Dr. Lonstein put a full-body cast on me during our second operation on my sixth birthday. One upside of having surgery on my birthday was the operating room nurses sang "Happy Birthday" before I drifted off to another anesthesia-induced sleep. After I woke up in my hospital room, I saw a Happy Birthday banner on the ceiling. This was definitely my worst birthday ever, but it was necessary in order for me to see my seventh birthday.

I regained some lung capacity by inhaling air using a spirometer several times a day. Less than a week after my birthday, I was cleared by Dr. Lonstein to go home. Wearing a seat belt jacket, I laid down on the backseat during the three-day road trip to Florida. Every few hours, we had to pull over so my parents could turn me and change my position to prevent pneumonia and soreness.

I wore the cast and halo for over three months, an eternity to a six-year-old. Mom tried to make me feel better by reminding me that angels have halos, which helped a little. One day, Mom pulled me, halo and all, in my red Radio Flyer™ wagon two blocks to the library where I proudly received my first library card. We happily checked out several books to read and tapes to watch at home.

Three times a day, my pin sites had to be cleaned with distilled water, hydrogen peroxide, and iodine to prevent infection. By the time the halo was removed, my parents had gone through 6,000 sterile Q-Tips™. After Mom ordered the Q-Tips™ from a local medical supply company, two representatives from the store delivered them and other items to our house with a question.

"We were wondering why you ordered so many Q-Tips™," said one of the representatives. "Are you doing something to get into the Guinness Book of World Records?"

"Not this week," said Mom, chuckling. "I need the Q-Tips™ to clean my daughter's halo pin sites and prevent infection."

The surgery and recovery resulted in a reduction in my scoliosis, which eliminated the risk of collapsed lungs. However, we later discovered I needed instrumentation in my back to keep it straight.

Subsequently, Dr. Lonstein performed another operation on my spine in July of 1993. This surgery wasn't as involved as the previous one, but it further stabilized my spine and kept it straighter for a longer period of time. My parents and I were able to fly back and forth this time because I could sit since I only had to wear a back brace after surgery.

Before going home, my parents and I went to the Mall of America, the United States' largest mall. Along with over 500 stores, restaurants, and fun activities such as miniature golf and water toy boat races, my favorite attraction at the Mall of America was the Ferris wheel, which I rode with Dad. This is the only Ferris wheel I've been brave enough to ride.

My parents and I have returned to the Mall of America a few times since then. Over the years, we also went to a conservatory park, the Hubert H. Humphrey Metrodome, home of the Minnesota Vikings and Twins, and the state Capitol, where I saw Governor Jesse Ventura's office. A couple of times, I met with a girl from Minnesota who has the same disorder I do.

I appreciate how my parents made happy memories for me when we were in Minneapolis for not-so-happy purposes.

Hips and Hamstrings

In January of 1998, my parents and I flew to Baltimore to meet with an orthopedic surgeon named Dr. Steven Kopits whom I'd met in 1996 and 1997 in Orlando. A friend of mine with *campomelic syndrome* from Florida was a patient of his. Dr. Kopits, whose specialty was skeletal dysplasia, was very kind and enthusiastic about working on my right hip, which had dislocated, causing me pain, and my lower legs where the hamstrings had tightened once again from constantly sitting in my wheelchair.

My spine was experiencing more curvature, and my parents had to decide whether an operation was needed right away. Following consultation with doctors, the consensus was my back should be fixed before my hip. After a successful spine surgery in Minnesota in March and a family vacation in Buffalo in early July, my parents and I drove to Baltimore to begin a summer of surgeries.

The first of three major reconstructive surgeries came toward the end of July at St. Joseph's Medical Center in Towson, a suburb of Baltimore. This time in addition to an IV, I had Hemovac drain tubes in my legs to remove excess blood and fluids. After a couple of days, the Hemovac tubes were removed, which was an unpleasant experience.

The day after my surgery, Dad had to go back to Florida for work, but he kept in touch with me and returned to Baltimore several times during the summer.

At the end of the first week, I moved to Uncle John's apartment in Baltimore, where he had a hospital bed in the living room. Two weeks later, I went back to the hospital by ambulance for the next operation.

During the surgery, my right hip fell apart due to severe osteoporosis, but Dr. Kopits was able to put it back together with staples, wires, screws, and a compression plate. After a brief recovery, I went back to Uncle John's place again where relatives and friends came to visit throughout the summer.

Finally, I had my last orthopedic surgery with Dr. Kopits near the end of August. After each operation, I had to wear a hip spica cast. By the end of my third surgery, I had hardware in my right hip and both of my knees.

In September, more than two weeks after my third surgery, I went back to the operating room so Dr. Kopits could finish putting a cast on me while I was awake. He said this would prevent nighttime muscle spasms like the ones I had with my cast in 1994. Thankfully, he was right.

Dr. Kopits approved of my going home for the remainder of September and October. My parents drove me home, strapped down on the back seat with my cast on. Although this wasn't the summer vacation I had in mind, I'm thankful for the opportunity to bond with Uncle John in a way I wouldn't have otherwise.

One day during that summer while looking through an issue of the magazine *American Girl*, I read an article about Locks of Love, an organization that makes wigs for children with cancer. My hairdresser Rose, who has been making my hair look good since I was a preschooler, came to my house in late September and cut twelve inches of hair, which she sent to Locks of Love on my behalf.

Several weeks later, I received a thank-you note from Locks of Love. Despite being laid up in a cast, I felt glad to be of service to a child with cancer. I enjoyed donating hair so much I did it again in 2008, this time with the assistance of my Aunt Bonnie, who co-owns Tresses Salon in Hamburg, New York.

After wearing a cast for almost 100 days, I was on the road again with my parents, returning to Baltimore around Halloween (no more trick-or-treating for me) to have my cast removed and to begin almost three months of intense physical rehabilitation.

My excitement about the removal of my cast was short-lived. My legs felt so sore without it that tears came to my eyes. I had thought it would feel wonderful to move my legs freely, but they were stiff and painful without the support of the cast. Dad took me into a hot tub, on his lap, which relieved the pain somewhat and made washing off the dry skin on my legs easier.

Before starting physical rehabilitation, new AFO braces were made for my feet. Rehab involved swimming in the hospital pool, which I didn't enjoy very much because I feared I might inhale water. Nonetheless, swimming was an effective form of physical therapy for me.

During rehab, I contracted bronchitis; I must've been the happiest kid with bronchitis because I couldn't go into the pool for a week.

When I wasn't swimming, I was strapped while lying on my back to a tilt table to practice standing. I took my first steps with a walker and did other exercises with a nun named Sister Celeste, who introduced me to the game Mancala. I met a young man also going through rehab named Vincent DePaul (like the patron saint of charitable works). Little did I know I would be volunteering for an organization with the saint's name within the next few years.

Dr. Kopits was a beloved doctor who truly cared about his patients. One day during my rehab, he came to my hospital room while making his rounds. Nana, who flew to Baltimore in November, was with me at the time since Mom was resting at a guesthouse on the hospital property.

"How are you today, Ashley?" asked Dr. Kopits.

"I'm good," said I. "Nana and I are going to have a party tonight."

"I'm going to a party tonight, too," said Dr. Kopits.

After dinner, Nana and I were hanging out when Dr. Kopits entered my room wearing a tuxedo.

"Good evening, ladies," said Dr. Kopits. "May I join the party?"

"Sure, come on in!" said Nana and I. "You're a bit overdressed, but we're glad you came."

I admired Dr. Kopits's dedication to his patients.

Feeling homesick, I wanted to spend Thanksgiving with family in western New York for the first time ever. Taking my rehab progress into consideration, Dr. Kopits permitted me to do this. With Nana and me in tow, my parents drove to Buffalo. I was thankful for this mini-vacation that helped me forget about rehab for a few days.

I was also able to celebrate Christmas and the New Year in western New York. Before this mini-vacation, Mom, Grandma, Uncle John, and I slowly drove down 34th Street in Baltimore. Every house on this street was decked out for Christmas in honor of the movie *Miracle on 34th Street* (1947). The holiday spirit boosted my morale as I neared the end of rehab.

After the first of the year, Dad helped Mom and me get settled in at the Burkshire Hotel, which was located close to the hospital. During our first night there, while Mom carried me to the bedroom, she tripped over a bed spread. I flew out of her arms and made a soft landing on my mattress on the floor. Shaken, Mom crawled to me and made sure I wasn't hurt. Luckily, no bones were broken, and I was able to complete rehab.

In January of 1999, I was presented with a small trophy at a rehabilitation graduation party at the hospital. I was very glad to be done with rehab and be on my way home.

During my trips to Baltimore, my parents and I went to the Baltimore Zoo and Aquarium and took a tour of the White House and the Smithsonian in Washington, D.C. I didn't meet President George W. Bush, but it was wonderful to see some of the rooms in his place of residence.

I saw Dr. Kopits for follow-ups before he passed away from a brain tumor in 2002. Putting his patients before himself, he didn't live long enough to see the full impact of his work on my life. Dr. Kopits will never be forgotten.

Back in Palm Bay, I still had to keep up with my seventh grade studies throughout the 1998-1999 school year. This was made possible by a guidance counselor named Ms. Dean. She came to my house almost every day after work to go over with me what other seventh graders were learning. Once in a while, she brought me a McDonald's Happy Meal™ for dinner, which made me, well, happy!

I learned pre-algebra, English, world history, and science from Ms. Dean that year. For English, I read Thornton Wilder's play *Our Town*. The third and final act of the play changed my perspective on the concepts of death and eternity. I'll always appreciate Ms. Dean for getting me through seventh grade. If it weren't for her, I would've been a year behind schedule academically.

On a weekly basis for a few months, I had sessions with a physical therapist to maintain my strength. Before bed every night, my thighs were hooked up to an electrical stimulator. After a couple of months, I felt a sharp pain in my right hip. I had X-rays taken, and they showed one of the pins in my hip protruding more than the others. My parents and I decided to have the pin surgically removed. On the day before my thirteenth birthday, I went to the local hospital early in the morning. Fortunately, the procedure lasted less than an hour, and I was discharged by lunchtime. The pain in my hip subsided, and I was well enough to enjoy my birthday.

Shortly before my thirteenth birthday, Mom surprised me with a private drum lesson at home. This was a lot of fun for me because I've always been fascinated by percussion instruments despite my lack of musical talent. The gentleman who gave me the lesson was kind and patient with me and declined Mom's offer of payment at the end of our session.

Mom also hosted a party for my thirteenth birthday at home. We invited a few of my closest friends and their mothers for a mother/daughter-themed celebration that turned out to be lovely. Mom's thinking was as her daughter was approaching her teenage years, it's important to maintain a close bond with her child, and she wanted to share this with my friends and their moms. I liked this idea; it set the tone for my teenage years well.

I wish I didn't have to undergo intensive operations as a child, but they were necessary for the sake of my health. I'm grateful I haven't had a major surgery for over a decade.

Power to the Wheelchair!

During the later years of elementary school, I wished I had a power chair so I could control where I went without relying on a teacher or classmate to push me. In the spring of 1998, Mom, Nana, and I went to the Shriners' Hospital for Children in Tampa. The wheelchair technicians there did an assessment, and I tested out a power chair. It was anticipated this process at the hospital would take five days, but because of my eagerness to learn operation of the sample power chair, I was able to go home in two days.

Before we went home, Mom, Nana, and I spent a day at Busch Gardens to which I'd never been. While there, we rode on a train throughout the park, and an artist drew a caricature of my face that still hangs on my bedroom wall.

Due to my summer surgeries and recovery, I didn't receive my power chair until almost a year later. It was well worth the wait to gain a heightened sense of independence. My power chair was helpful when I started serving as a lector (reader) at my church in early June of 1999. Perhaps due to my gratitude for my recovery, I wanted to be more involved at church. I chose to read Bible passages to the congregation as opposed to joining the choir. Being tone deaf, my singing would clear out my church faster than you can say, "Hallelujah!"

I was also thankful to have my power chair for my Uncle Bobby's wedding in late June of 1999. As a junior bridesmaid, wearing a pink dress, I was able to participate in the procession with the bride's brother down the long aisle of Our Lady of Victory National Shrine & Basilica (which contains the United States' second largest dome) in Lackawanna, New York. The beauty of the Basilica and its decorations, including paintings and numerous statues of angels, amazed me.

In the summer of 2000, there was a family gathering at a cousin's home in Angola, New York. I nearly wore down the battery on my power chair that day exploring the property with my great Aunt Rose (Nana's sister). Despite the time I was bit by a goat, I bravely fed a horse hay before I followed Aunt Rose to one side of the land lined by trees with berries, a few of which we picked and ate.

Aunt Rose and I then came upon a pond where there was a flock of ducks by the water. I made my way toward the ducks, and one by one, they went into the water. I thought that was really cool. Finally, Aunt Rose and I went to a tennis court on the property, where I attempted to hit some balls with a racket. We also tossed around a Woosh Frisbee™. It was a fun day, enhanced by my power chair.

One unfortunate long-term outcome of sitting in a wheelchair is the loss of bone mass (osteoporosis). In my college years, I consulted with my endocrinologist, who prescribed a weekly dose of a medication which had no favorable results. Then, I switched to an annual IV infusion for the next five years, and my bone density did improve.

Weight-bearing exercise and daily supplements of vitamins D and K, with calcium will also help to prevent further bone mass deterioration.

I had many adventures with my first power chair, which made me feel more self-sufficient. I still have a manual wheelchair for rainy (and snowy) days, rough terrain, and inaccessible houses, but my preferred means of transportation is my power chair.

Mom's Fifteen Minutes of Fame

The first talk show I watched on a regular basis was *The Rosie O'Donnell Show* starting in 1996. Rosie temporarily took her show from New York City to Universal Studios' Islands of Adventure in Orlando in May of 1999. My former babysitter Rikki and I signed up for tickets and, between the two of us, received invitations to attend three tapings.

Mom and I went to the first taping together on Monday, May 10, the day after Mother's Day. Country singer Wynonna Judd was a guest. After the show, I met Rosie, who signed my Rosie O'Doll and posed with me for a photo. My smile in this photo is bigger than that of the Cheshire Cat! I was fortunate to have that moment with Rosie because she didn't do any more meet-and-greets that week. As if that wasn't exciting enough, there's more.

Mom didn't see the need to go back to Orlando for the second taping because she didn't think it'd be better than our first experience, but I convinced her. On May 12, we took Nana with us, which turned out to be a good thing because she assisted Mom with me. While we were waiting in line, Rosie's producers approached Mom about a chance to play a game on the show. At first, Mom didn't really want to do it, but Nana and I talked her into it.

One of the guests on Rosie's show that day was Emmy Award-winning actress Camryn Manheim, who rode into the studio on her motorcycle. After Rosie's interview with Camryn, it was Mom's turn to shine. Following the unveiling of the prize, a 2000 Chevrolet Cavalier, Rosie called Mom onto the stage to play a game called "The Big Ro Throw."

"Tracy, what do you do?" asked Rosie after Mom introduced herself.

"I take care of your #1 fan, my daughter Ashley," said Mom with pride.

After this conversation ended, Camryn unsuccessfully attempted to win the car for Mom by throwing three oranges toward the mouth on a large cardboard replica of Rosie's face. In front of 2,000 people in the studio audience, not to mention millions of home viewers, Mom grabbed an orange, stepped up to the line, and threw with her right hand. On only her second try, Mom's orange flew through the paper into the mouth on Rosie's big cardboard head. Then, there was pandemonium: Mom raised her arms in victory; Rosie screamed happily and jumped up and down; Camryn (like a true entertainer) juggled oranges; and the crowd went wild as confetti fell. Sitting next to me in the handicapped section of the audience, Nana cried tears of joy while I yelled, "That's my mom! That's my mom!"

Standing on stage, Mom looked in my direction and signed the words "I love you." She had to calm Rosie down and take the show to a commercial break by announcing the band N*SYNC was coming on next. By the way, Mom was the only audience member that week to win the car on her own; the other contestants were assisted after they threw three oranges. Rosie was quick to point this fact out by exclaiming, "You won for real!"

It was evident Mom still had a little athletic ability from her younger years. Mom's winning the car on *The Rosie O'Donnell Show* is definitely one of the top ten moments of Mom's and my lives. She generously gave the car to Dad, but she drives it once in a while. To this day, whenever she throws something into a trash can from several feet away without dropping it, Mom declares, "This arm wins cars!"

Mom, Nana, and I went back to Orlando the following day for a third taping in which the late actor Patrick Swayze was a guest. This time, we got to sit in the front row. I interacted with Rosie again and received a Rosie show jean jacket. I attended three more show tapings in Orlando over the next two years, and Rosie recognized me every time.

Her talk show ended in 2002, and I've followed Rosie's career since then. One of my favorite movies in which she starred is *A League of Their Own* (1992). Watching the pitcher in that movie reminds me of Mom's throwing oranges on Rosie's show.

Chapter 5

Changing Directions at Southwest Middle

"Y2K turned out to be A-OK."

I felt exhilarated to go back to school for the eighth grade at Southwest Middle School, less than a mile from my house. I enjoyed Southwest so much I even went to school when it was closed for a day due to a tropical storm because I didn't know about the closure ahead of time. The assistant principal thought this was pretty funny.

From Drama to Science Research

For my elective, I decided to take a Drama class because I thought I had the potential to be a unique actress. After all, I was in a few plays in elementary school (including my breakout roles in "Goldilocks" and "Mrs. Sun"). I enjoyed reading books (including plays) out loud, and I was complimented often by my teachers on how well I read in class. So, I thought, why not give drama a try? Mom, who was in a couple of musicals in high school, liked the idea of being a stage mother, so she approved my choice.

For someone who used to receive speech therapy, I did rather well in Drama for a couple of weeks. My teacher appeared to be impressed with my performance. However, not many students had registered for the Science Research class in which students prepared for a science fair to be held the following semester. To generate more interest in the class, my science teacher Ms. McCormick offered the maximum amount of extra credit to students who signed up for Science Research. Since I was obsessed with extra credit, this was all the convincing I needed to switch classes, so I bade farewell to Drama and said hello to Science Research.

It ended up being a good move because I won second place in the Biochemistry category at the south Brevard County Science Fair for my project about the type of orange juice that contained the highest amount of Vitamin C. Dad went to Southwest with me during a few weekends to assist me with my project, which involved titration to determine Vitamin C levels in the different orange juices. Ironically, I had a cold when finishing my project and giving practice presentations to several students and teachers, and laryngitis made it more difficult to speak. My interest in science stayed with me, and I studied social sciences at college.

Another bonus of participating in the science fair was I met Joyce Good Henderson (a local author and nurse) and her daughter Heather, who collaborated on a book about science fair projects. They included a little information about my project in their book, and I was honored to be one of the individuals to whom they dedicated their book.

When I developed a serious interest in writing during high school, Joyce offered to be my writing mentor for which I'm very grateful.

Learning and Lunch in History

Having developed a bit of an interest in history encouraged by both of my grandfathers, I enjoyed learning about wars, presidents, and other facts from my American history teacher Ms. Howser. My classmates and I were assigned to read Michael Shaara's *Killer Angels*, a novel about the Battle of Gettysburg in 1863. We then completed projects based on the book. This assignment inspired my parents and me to make a side trip to Gettysburg, Pennsylvania, while visiting Uncle John in Baltimore.

Wanting to ensure I was being well cared for after my surgeries the previous year, Mom served as my assistant at school during the eighth grade. She arranged for me to eat lunch while lying down on a tilt table in Ms. Howser's classroom so I could stretch my legs and rest my body. I would've rather eaten lunch and socialized with my friends in the cafeteria like I did in elementary school, but this was a good opportunity for me to get out of my wheelchair and relax.

G.B., a gifted boy from my class, also stayed in the classroom for lunch, usually doing homework or studying. One day, he brought his flute with him. Mom and I asked him to play a song for us, and he did. G.B. was so intelligent but self-critical, and whenever he was frustrated about something, he would mutter, "Damn it!"

Having been raised not to swear, I was shocked at first to hear G.B. speak this way, but I got used to it after a while. He moved away after the eighth grade but reappeared at my high school less than a year later. He wrote a very nice note in my yearbook that makes me smile whenever I read it. This is the note:

"Ashley, you're an incredible, resilient person. I've had the utmost respect for you ever since our first meeting in Ms. Bowden's class. You show such tenacity when applying yourself it makes me ashamed when I procrastinate. Keep striving for your dreams and have an excellent summer!"

This boy knew how to make a girl feel good about herself! G.B. completed high school early and enrolled at the Florida Institute of Technology during my senior year. Sadly, he passed away at the beginning of the fall semester in 2004. The connection he and I had was nothing more than friendship, but I sometimes wonder if our relationship could've gone beyond that. I still think about him fondly.

Only Time Would Tell

After Christmas in 1999, the celebratory tone of the holidays quickly changed to one of anxiety and confusion. People all over the world were fearful about the end of the millennium. They acted as if a natural disaster was on the way by going to grocery stores and stocking up on food and water. I heard from the media about Y2K, including the possibility of computers (and machines operated by them) malfunctioning. Formerly an exciting occasion that was celebrated with much fanfare by many people while others observed it quietly, the end of the year had never been so stressful on a global scale. I think the New Year's resolution of the people afraid of Y2K was to just survive. As a thirteen-year-old, I wasn't sure what to make of Y2K, but I didn't feel like my family and I were in danger.

To celebrate the approach of the new millennium, Grandma wanted her six children, their spouses, and eight grandchildren (ranging in age from four to thirteen) to spend New Year's Eve with her and Grandpa at their house near Buffalo, New York. Since my parents and I lived in Florida, it wasn't too often our extended family was all under one roof. After hearing about what may be the end of the world, I didn't know if this would be our final celebration, but I knew this family gathering was a treat and would be enjoyable regardless.

The family and I kicked off New Year's Eve by celebrating Aunt Carol's birthday, which happens to be December 31. We gathered around the dining room table and ate dinner followed by cake and ice cream. Throughout the night, Grandpa took pictures of us to commemorate the occasion. We found out my aunt wouldn't be the only one to receive a gift that night from my grandparents. They gave their children VHS tapes made from their childhood home movies.

Dad and his younger siblings were pleasantly surprised. Considering Grandpa often took pictures of us, it didn't surprise me he had recorded these home movies as well. We immediately began watching the home movies, which brought back happy memories and made the evening pass quickly. I thought it was neat to see my dad growing up during the 1950s and '60s in the very house in which we were celebrating New Year's Eve. Before watching the home movies, I had thought of Dad only as a grown man, so I was glad I had the chance to see how he started out in life. I was also amazed to see how young my grandparents looked.

Before we knew it, the new millennium was upon us. At the stroke of midnight, I waited with bated breath to see what was going to happen. After a moment, I realized everything appeared to be okay. The world didn't come to an end. The electricity was still on, and the clocks continued to tick. As my grandparents and their children kissed and hugged, my cousins and I wished each other a happy new year and celebrated with colorful noisemakers before going to bed.

I learned later there were minor glitches in some places with the changing of the year from 1999 to 2000, but otherwise, Y2K turned out to be A-OK. I realize now it was silly for people to be so scared. However, it's better to be overly prepared than unprepared. This was one of my most memorable New Year's Eve celebrations for only positive reasons. I'll treasure this memory for the rest of my life. I wonder if people in 2999 will have fears about the end of that year, assuming their lives on Earth (or elsewhere) will revolve around technology like in the cartoon *The Jetsons* (1962-1987).

Ashley and the Bee

One of the best days of eighth grade was the day I won the school spelling bee after correctly spelling the word *statuesque*. I worked really hard to prepare for the bee because I came closer and closer to winning from fourth to sixth grades. Every time I was told what word to spell, I acted like the spellers at the annual Scripps National Spelling Bee shown on television and asked for everything related to the word I was allowed to know (its definition, its use in a sentence, its language of origin, etc.).

The first time I did this, the surprised teacher had to go get a dictionary, but by my next turn, the teacher was ready for my line of questioning. I ended up being the Southwest Middle School Spelling Bee champion, one of my goals in the eighth grade.

After the bee ended, I went to my English class where my late teacher Viola Bowden and my classmates were. Thinking I had lost the spelling bee since I returned sooner than expected, Ms. Bowden started to console me before I told her I won. A prim and proper woman from Massachusetts, Ms. Bowden was so elated about my good news she was practically jumping up and down in her high heels and dress. We hugged, and she announced to my classmates she was going to keep her promise about bringing doughnuts to class to celebrate my victory. How sweet it was!

This victory advanced me to the county spelling bee at the school board building in Viera, Florida, weeks later. My parents and grandparents were in the audience. Unfortunately, I was eliminated during the first round because I misheard the word I was supposed to spell (ruddy) despite a few repetitions of the word. Here's a way to use the word *ruddy* in a sentence: Ashley had a ruddy complexion on her face when she was eliminated from the spelling bee. I was humiliated and disappointed, but I was still proud of achieving my initial goal of winning the school spelling bee.

Battle of the Books

As if I didn't have enough books to read with all of my classes, I chose to sign up for the Sunshine State Readers Battle of the Books. To be eligible for this, I had to read a few books that were on a list distributed by the school librarian and answer several questions about them during a preliminary session.

After making the cut along with five other students, I was required to choose three books to read thoroughly so I'd be familiar with them. I also had to make up questions about the books and record their answers. Due to my love of reading, I read all of the books while focusing on three of them. My favorite book for the Battle was Dan Gutman's *Honus & Me*, which was about a boy's discovery of a valuable Honus Wagner baseball card.

I learned the meaning of irony from the outcome of the Battle of the Books. During the week before this event, I noticed one of the authors' names was printed incorrectly on the required reading list. In an effort to prevent the confusion of my teammates, I brought this to the librarian's attention, and she said she would inform my teammates of this error.

I didn't know how crucial the error would be until the night of the Battle of the Books. At this event, teams from local schools gathered to answer numerous questions about the books we were required to read. If a team lost two rounds, the team was out of the competition. My team lost the first round, so we realized this was going to be harder than we thought. Fortunately, we had a bye for the second round, so we were able to take a short break and regroup before the third round. Then, we won every round until the final round.

During the final round, we were asked a question about the author's name of the book I had pointed out to the school librarian (I swear I'm not making this up). I hoped the boy who was the expert of that book was told about the author's name. Unfortunately, he wasn't, for he kept saying to the team the book's author was Clifton G. Wisler when it was actually G. Clifton Wisler. I tried my darnedest to convince him he wasn't saying the author's name correctly, but he wouldn't budge. He gave his answer, and alas, it was wrong. The other team was confused, so its members also answered incorrectly. After the correct answer was revealed, the team captain turned to me with a sad look on her face and apologized for not listening to me. We ended up losing that round, so we were awarded second place, which was Southwest's best performance at the Battle of the Books up to that point.

And the Award Goes to….

In the spring of 2000, my algebra teacher Mrs. Hansell informed me she had nominated me for a WonderKid award because of my academic achievements and excellent behavior. Then, she told me my application was accepted. We were invited to attend an awards ceremony near WonderWorks, a museum in Orlando.

A local prominent lawyer presided over the ceremony since he was the CEO of WonderWorks. I received several items in addition to a WonderKid certificate. After the ceremony, my parents, Mrs. Hansell, and I ate a delicious dinner at the Cracker Barrel. This was another wonderful (pun intended) memory for me from middle school.

On a rainy night at the end of the school year, Southwest's annual awards ceremony took place. It still makes me giggle when I think about Dad and the assistant principal lifting my power chair onto the sidewalk to avoid getting my chair wet in a puddle by the curb cut. Little did I know how memorable this evening would be for me as well as my loved ones.

First of all, I was presented with a plaque for my role on the Sunshine State Readers Battle of the Books team and another plaque for getting straight A's, both of which still hang above my bedroom door. I was also given a certificate and a medallion for winning the school spelling bee.

The biggest surprise of the night came at the end of the ceremony. A woman from the local Chamber of Commerce approached the podium and began describing a student that sounded a lot like me. When I realized I was about to receive one of the most prestigious awards for eighth graders, my heart started pounding. I was so excited when the Chamber representative finally announced my name and presented me with the Student Leadership Award, a small gold-colored trophy, which still sits on a mantel in my room.

Eighth grade was unforgettable also because I attended my first dance. I didn't have a date, but I still had a good time dancing and socializing with a group of classmates while my parents chaperoned. I wasn't concerned about how I looked when I moved to the music. The dance was a fun way for me to spend a Friday night.

For part of the school year, a club in which I participated was the Family, Career and Community Leaders of America (FCCLA), which encourages members' development of important life skills. I was drawn to this organization because it reminded me of 4-H. FCCLA reinforced my desire to be involved in the community.

I made up for missing the seventh grade.

Chapter 6

Wheeling Around the Real Bayside High

"The speed of the race cars resembled how quickly four years of high school went by for me."

Saved by the Bell (1989-1993) was one of my favorite TV shows while I was growing up. I had a crush on actor Mario Lopez, who played Slater on the show. On Christmas at my grandparents' house one year, I woke up in the middle of the night with a nasty stomach virus and a fever. I was bummed to be sick, but receiving the *Saved by the Bell* board game later that day cheered me up.

Coincidentally, Bayside was the name of both the high school on the TV show and my high school in Palm Bay. Comparisons can be made between the fictional and real Baysides: (1) At TV's Bayside, Mr. Tuttle was a teacher. At my Bayside, Mr. Tuttle was the principal. (2) At TV's Bayside, Kelly and Zack dated before getting married years later. At my Bayside, Kelly and Zack were just friends. (3) At TV's Bayside, there was a character with the nickname Screech. At my Bayside, *screech* was the sound the wheels on my power chair made whenever I made a turn in the hallway.

Freshman Year

Around this time, my parents decided to make a few modifications to our ranch-style house to improve its accessibility. A representative from the local independent living center completed a home assessment. To make wheeling over thresholds easier, we purchased portable ramps.

Dad installed a new bathroom countertop with an accessible sink, and helped a contractor install a wheel-in shower.

With the exception of electives, the classes on my schedule were taught at the honors level. My first high school teacher was John Tucker, who taught American Government one semester and Economics the other semester. Mr. Tucker tried to portray himself as a tough guy by warning me on the first day he was mean, but he was a good-natured man with a sense of humor. I can only imagine the teasing he endured when the movie *John Tucker Must Die* came out in 2006.

In Biology, I learned about the anatomy of a piglet through dissection. Seeing it as a learning experience, this activity didn't gross me out, but my biology partner had a harder time dealing with it. With my classmate's capable hands and my words of encouragement, we got through dissection together.

I also took Newspaper as well as Business Systems and Technology with Mrs. Kraus. She agrees with me my best newspaper headline was "Lord Is Here to Guide," an article I wrote about a new guidance counselor whose surname was Lord. Mrs. Kraus was also the advisor of Bayside's chapter of the Future Business Leaders of America (FBLA) of which I was historian for one year and vice president for three years. During my college years, I served as a speech timer and guest speaker at FBLA events.

I knew upon entering high school I would need to appear as a well-rounded student on my résumé. I joined the Chess Club, sponsored by Mr. Tucker, because it was an intellectual game I wanted to learn. My fellow members and I started out playing chess with the best of intentions, but one day, someone brought the board game Risk™ to a meeting. After that distraction, no one besides me seemed interested in chess anymore, so I decided to move on to other activities.

It was during high school I learned the value of volunteering. Due to a full-ride college scholarship for which I was applying, I was required to volunteer for 100 hours. I began volunteering for the Society of St. Vincent de Paul at my church by collecting monetary donations for the food pantry. Starting in my junior year when I took Pre-calculus, I stayed after school once a week to tutor math students. I also volunteered at a few community events such as March of Dimes walkathons.

Keeping the Faith at School

In January of 2001, I received the sacrament of Confirmation after attending weekly classes for a year. As my sponsor, Nana (also my godmother) stood with me when I was confirmed by the Bishop of the Diocese of Orlando. I also had the honor of reading a Bible passage during the Mass.

Not long after my Confirmation, a junior student invited me to join the Fellowship of Christian Athletes (FCA). I accepted her invitation and attended a meeting where I noticed a few teenagers from my church. The sponsor Mrs. Townsend and the members made me feel welcome despite my not being an athlete. Later in the year, Mrs. Townsend told me about an opportunity to go to an FCA leadership camp on a scholarship during the summer.

In the spring, Grandma, Grandpa, and Uncle Jim from Pennsylvania came to Florida for a visit. Together, we attended a Los Angeles Dodgers spring training baseball game at Holman Stadium in Vero Beach, Florida. My family and I spotted *America's Most Wanted* (1988-2013) host John Walsh with a boy we assumed to be his youngest son sitting a few rows in front of us. We didn't disturb them, but I saw a few people walk up to him and start a conversation. Perhaps tired of being approached by other people, John and his son left before the game ended. You just never know who you'll see when out and about.

In June, Mom and I went to the FCA camp in St. Simons Island, Georgia, where we stayed for a week at a hotel on the campgrounds while the other campers slept in cabins. This was truly one of the best weeks of my life. Each day at camp (which contained an atmosphere of kindness and solidarity) began with calisthenics and breakfast in the cafeteria. Throughout the day, there were workshops, athletic activities, shared meals, and camp meetings that included energizing and uplifting Christian music.

I was part of a huddle with other high school girls and a young woman who served as our leader. We met as a group twice a day; our meetings consisted of prayer, Bible readings, and discussions. I still have my FCA Bible with the girls' contact information in it. In a display of team spirit, the girls and I came up with a chant we would say before each athletic event. The chant went something like this: "We're the girls from Huddle 15! We're the best team you've ever seen. We don't care if we win. We're here to worship Him!"

By the end of the week, the girls in my huddle and I formed a bond. I made up for not being an athlete by displaying team spirit and cheering loudly for my teammates during daily athletic challenges. I was able to participate in the final event of the week: a relay race. One of my teammates pushed me in a wheelchair for several yards to the next point in the relay. She pushed me so quickly I felt the wheelchair shaking and heard it rattling, but I was happy to be in the race. During the final camp meeting, I was one of two campers out of over 400 to receive the Sportsmanship Award, a small star-shaped trophy. As my huddle leader pushed me to the stage to receive the award, everyone began chanting my name: "Ashley! Ashley! Ashley!"

I felt like the MVP of a sporting event. The camp motivated me to become more involved with FCA by being secretary of Bayside's chapter and participating in student-run Christian events before and after school. The FCA leadership camp also gave me a sense of peace and encouragement I needed before my last major surgery, which was performed on my spine by Dr. Lonstein in Minneapolis on July 9, 2001.

This surgery was necessary to correct spine curvature due to my continued growth and to relieve back pain. The doctor removed a portion of the support rods that were no longer needed. I was taken off the respirator the next day, and the first thing I did with a raspy voice was wish Dad a happy birthday since his birthday is July 10. Grandma and Aunt Carol came from Buffalo, and they stayed with Mom at the women's shelter. I recovered quickly and was able to go back to school the following month for my sophomore year.

Sophomore Year

The day known as 9/11 occurred when I was fifteen years old in 2001. Instead of doing class work, my newspaper classmates and I watched in disbelief the footage of the airplanes crashing into the World Trade Center. I didn't have any relatives or friends who died on that day, but I was nonetheless aware of the gravity of the situation. The number of people who died due to this act of terrorism was staggering, and the destruction of the Twin Towers was also heartbreaking. As a display of patriotism, I decided to include the American flag in the design of my high school class ring.

My English teacher was Mrs. Stephenson, who also taught Advanced Placement (AP) Language my junior year. At that time, *American Idol* was a popular show. In preparation for the AP exam, my classmates and I had to write numerous essays under timed conditions throughout the school year. Most of our essays were returned to us with a lot of comments, some of which were not so good.

Due to Mrs. Stephenson's constant criticism, she was dubbed by my classmates "Simon of AP" after Simon Cowell, a former *American Idol* judge. Looking back at it, I know she meant well; she was just trying to prepare us for the AP exam so we could pass it. And I did pass, thanks to Mrs. Stephenson and her red pen.

Taking a foreign language course was mandatory, so I chose Spanish because I thought it would be useful since there are many Hispanic people at my church. After all, the name of the state of Florida is Spanish. I did so well in Spanish class my teacher Señor Altamar, who was from Colombia, feared I was getting bored, so he encouraged me to write homework assignments for my classmates. I enjoyed learning Spanish and think it is a beautiful language that sometimes comes in handy.

I had Newspaper and Business once again with Mrs. Kraus. I was assigned to be the boys' golf team reporter. One of the boys on that team was Billy Horschel, who later became a professional golfer. Perhaps because of my work with the boys' golf team, I received a scholarship from the local golf course, which was ironic considering I only played miniature golf and golf video games.

I had Algebra 2 with Ms. Nguyen. One day, I played Connect Four™ with her in class. She beat me and several other students who challenged her, but I like to think I gave her a run for her money. Ms. Nguyen moved away after the school year ended.

For the final period of the day, I had Chemistry with Mrs. Wilson, who is now Dr. Wilson. During the first semester, Mrs. Wilson looked for students to help her with her project called Chemistry for Kids. The purpose of this program was to increase interest in science among fourth graders. This sounded appealing to me because I completed an award-winning science project in the fourth grade. I signed up and am glad I did because it was a lot of fun and rewarding to see the fourth graders' interest in science increase. We traveled in groups of four to local elementary schools and gave chemistry presentations that included dry ice, colored carnations, and Silly String™.

At the end of the school year, Mrs. Wilson wrote a heartfelt message in my yearbook. Part of the note says, "You are my inspiration. You are the reason I decided to start a new career."

I was touched but rather surprised by her note. Mrs. Wilson didn't quit teaching because of her hour-long commute. She didn't quit because of a student who put liquid soap in her aquarium, thereby killing her fish. She quit because of *me*!

Actually, what she meant was she admired my ability to overcome obstacles, which led to her decision to become a pharmacist. She proceeded to obtain a doctorate and began her new career by the time of my community college graduation four years later. We still keep in touch today.

In the spring semester, I was inducted into the National Honor Society (NHS) in a ceremony held in the school cafeteria. The following year, I was elected treasurer of Bayside's NHS chapter. I attended a statewide conference in Orlando as an officer from my school. I had to get up earlier on the morning of an NHS meeting because it was held before school. That was worth it, though, because the NHS values of scholarship, leadership, service, and character have stayed with me.

For my Sweet Sixteen birthday celebration, I had a professional tea party with a few of my friends at home. This was a lovely idea considering my British heritage on Mom's side of the family. A woman wearing a bonnet told us about the history of tea parties and served us finger sandwiches and chocolate-covered potato chips along with cups of tea. It was much better than the tea parties my friends and I pretended to have with our stuffed animals when we were little girls.

During my high school years, Brevard County had a semi-professional basketball team called the Blue Ducks. During its first year, the team played home games at Bayside's gym. The game my parents and I attended was memorable. That day, the Blue Ducks competed against a team coached by retired NBA player Kareem Abdul-Jabbar.

When I was a kid, I thought Dad was tall at six feet, but he looked short next to Mr. Abdul-Jabbar at seven feet two inches. Although the Blue Ducks defeated his team, Mr. Abdul-Jabbar was gracious enough to stick around after the game for meet-and-greets. He autographed my tenth grade yearbook, which I think is cool.

Junior Year

Mom had been assisting me at Bayside for the past two years. Not that I didn't appreciate her assistance, but I wanted to be more independent. I decided to have a personal assistant provided by the school. In came Mrs. Pappas whose son was in Bayside's first graduating class. It didn't take long for Mrs. Pappas and me to become friends. She assisted me during my senior year, too.

"Crash" was one of Mrs. Pappas's nicknames for me despite my efforts to avoid crashing into anything or anyone with my wheelchair. This wasn't the first time I was called "Crash;" my Aunt Heidi called me this years earlier.

I had my last high school science course, Physics, with Bryan LaRose, who moved to the Caribbean after the end of the school year and tragically died less than a year later. For fourth period, I took a Health/PE class with Mrs. Townsend. Interestingly enough, there was a Health teacher at Bayside named Mrs. McGrath (no relation), but I chose to take the class with Mrs. Townsend since I knew her from FCA. While my PE classmates worked out in the school gym, I played adaptive sports with a personal coach. I felt fitter while having fun at the same time. Then, Mr. Tucker was my teacher once again, this time for AP World History.

During the first week of my Spanish 2 class with Señora Guzman from Puerto Rico, my classmates and I had to pick a Spanish name for ourselves. We were supposed to write this name down on all of our assignments and test papers. I chose the name *Cristina* because I had a couple of friends named Christina, and most of the letters in the name *Cristo* (Spanish for "Christ") are in *Cristina*. Therefore, my Spanish alter ego from August 2002 to May 2003 was Cristina McGrath. Señora Guzman even wrote my Spanish name in my school yearbook.

In January of 2003, Señora Guzman submitted my name to the United States Achievement Academy due to my excellent performance in her class. My photo and a few words about my accomplishments were printed in a national yearbook.

Grandma came up with the idea of taking a spring family vacation, so we spent time at a rental home in the Outer Banks of North Carolina during the week of Easter in April of 2003. The beachfront house named Twisted Fish was located in Nags Head on a barrier island bordering the Atlantic Ocean. It was large and had all the amenities you could think of, including a pool and two hot tubs. It even contained an elevator, which was perfect for me.

My family and I attended Easter Mass at a small church, went fishing, and visited lighthouses and Kitty Hawk, where the Wright brothers flew the first flight on an airplane a century earlier. I had to make time to do homework daily because I missed five days of school for this trip. Nevertheless, we all had a fun and memorable time.

During the summer before my senior year, I decided to take my first college course to meet my scholarship requirements. Along with three of my high school classmates, I enrolled in an introductory psychology class at the Palm Bay campus of Brevard Community College (renamed Eastern Florida State College in 2013). It was a positive experience for a first-time college student. The instructor was a psychologist who illustrated psychological concepts by referring to some of her clients anonymously.

The homework assignments were manageable, and I performed well on tests. My high school classmates and I completed a class project, which included a Bingo-style game with psychology vocabulary. This experience made me look forward to college even more, but I had to finish high school first.

My Moment with a Talking Bush

In May 2003, I attended the Family Café, an annual conference held at a hotel in the Orlando area for people with disabilities and their loved ones. The conference, which included various workshops and vendors, featured the Governor's Summit on Disabilities. Jeb Bush, President George W. Bush's brother, delivered the keynote address and graciously took time to meet-and-greet. During my moment with Governor Bush, he paid close attention to what I had to say. I was pleased to see a politician who had a genuine interest in citizens with disabilities.

I'm not the only member of my family who made contact with a Bush. During my freshman year of high school, Mom went to a rally at the Melbourne International Airport, where presidential candidate George W. Bush made a campaign stop. As he made his way to the podium, Bush quickly touched the hands of the people directly behind a rope, including Mom's. Years before that, Nana and Papa vacationed in Kennebunkport, Maine. Papa told us one day when he was golfing with a friend, he noticed former president George H. W. Bush from a distance. Papa saw President Bush drop a towel and promptly told him about it. Bush waved and thanked him. This encounter was as special as the two holes-in-one Papa shot in central Florida during his retirement years.

Senior Year

Senior year was without question the best year of high school for me. It started off with a bang when I was named Student of the Month by the local Chamber of Commerce in September of 2003. Accompanied by my parents, principal Mr. Tuttle, and guidance counselor Mrs. Sawyer, I received a plaque at a breakfast awards ceremony.

For AP Literature, my teacher was Ms. Shane (now Dr. Shane). She asked if she could interview me for one of her assignments for her Doctoral degree. I was flattered. Not surprisingly, she received an A on her assignment.

A neat coincidence took place years later when Ms. Shane received her doctorate on the same day I received my Master's degree from the

University of Central Florida (UCF) in August, 2010.

My love of literature extended beyond school; at age seventeen, I became a member of the Space Coast Writers' Guild due to an invitation from my writing mentor Joyce. Over the next two years, I edited submissions to the guild's literary magazine and presented a workshop to elementary school students. Due to the demands of college and my job search, I took an eight-year hiatus from the guild before returning.

An elective I took in the fall semester of my senior year involved serving as an assistant for Bayside's guidance department. My sole classmate and I, with Mrs. Pappas in tow, took turns delivering messages to teachers' classrooms and picking up mail from the front office. All of this transport made my power chair battery wear down more quickly than usual. When there were no deliveries, there was always office work to be completed such as stuffing envelopes and stapling or hole-punching stacks of paper. I learned a few skills from this class that have been useful in an office setting.

During the spring semester, I took an aerobics class. While my classmates exercised to a video tape, I followed my personalized exercise regimen, which included lifting barbells and stretching. Our final class project required us to create an exercise routine with appropriate music in the background. I was initially nervous about this assignment because my using a wheelchair limited the exercises I could do, but I knew it was possible because of Richard Simmons's exercise videos.

The only choice I had was to focus on exercises that can be done sitting on a chair. My routine included the songs "(Let's Get) Physical" by Olivia Newton-John and Buster Poindexter's rendition of Arrow's "Hot Hot Hot" and props like black and teal (my school colors) pom-poms. I was relieved when my aerobics teacher said my exercise routine was the best she'd ever seen. Her compliment boosted confidence in my ability to exercise despite my physical disabilities.

However, I didn't return to physical therapy for a decade because of my college schedule and being turned off from exercise by the intensity of the physical rehabilitation I underwent at age twelve. My experience shows exercise is important and possible for people with physical disabilities.

During the last week of school, my aerobics teacher gave my classmates and me permission to do whatever we wanted as long as we were quiet. She brought card games like Uno™ for those who wanted to play. I considered myself a skilled Uno™ player because I played it often during vacations in Buffalo. So, I decided to challenge my teacher to a game of Uno™ just for fun. Unlike when I played Connect Four™ with my algebra teacher two years before, I was victorious in Uno™ against my aerobics teacher. Fortunately, my teacher was a good sport, and I still got an A in aerobics.

For sixth period, I took Accounting 1 with none other than Mrs. Kraus with whom I was on the school newspaper staff for a third year. The information from this class helped me obtain the highest score on the Accounting 1 test at the FBLA district competition. Mrs. Kraus was elated because I was the first Bayside student to win first place in Accounting.

Prior to this, I had won first place in the public speaking category three years in a row and second place at the state competition during my freshman year, so I wasn't too sure about going outside my comfort zone. I'm glad I did in this case. I participated in the FBLA state competition at the Peabody Orlando for the last time on my eighteenth birthday. The Peabody was unique because every day back then, a red carpet was rolled out for a flock of ducks that took an elevator and marched to a fountain on the first floor while being observed by guests. A little birdie (or was it one of the ducks?) told the conference keynote speaker it was my birthday. I was pleasantly surprised he wished me a happy birthday at the beginning of his speech.

During my childhood, I wore back braces and braces on my feet due to deformed bones. When I was a senior in high school, I chose to wear braces on my teeth, which were crooked and crowded in my small mouth. I wanted a nicer smile like my parents, but I was apprehensive about how it would feel to have braces on my teeth for an extended period of time. Fortunately, my orthodontist listened to my concerns and made the process of having braces a smooth one. My braces were taken off in 2006, and I was given a retainer to wear. Although my braces cost a few thousand dollars, I feel like I have a million-dollar smile, which to me is priceless.

I wanted to participate in as many senior year events as my disabilities would allow. While preoccupied with my studies and extracurricular activities, I took time to observe school sporting events. Despite our busy schedules, Dad and I attended every home football game on Friday nights. We were allowed to view the games on the track, and I wouldn't leave before the school band marched away from the bleachers.

Mrs. Pappas was the coach of Bayside's junior varsity cheerleaders, who nominated me for homecoming queen. I wasn't selected to be part of the homecoming court, but it was still an honor to be nominated.

Each day during Spirit Week leading up to the homecoming dance, there was a theme such as "American Spirit Day" and "Hero Day," giving students the option of dressing up accordingly. I made an effort to show school spirit in my attire every day. Because of this, I was selected as the most spirited senior and awarded the privilege of sitting with two of my friends in front of the bleachers during the homecoming game. My friends and I were treated to chicken wings and other items from Beef 'O' Brady's, a local sports bar and restaurant. Later in the year, I was presented with a Bayside T-shirt on the school TV for continued academic excellence and school involvement.

The night after the football game, my homecoming dance date, a boy I'd known since the eighth grade, and I went to the Olive Garden for dinner with other dance attendees. From there, we proceeded to the homecoming dance at a local civic center where the theme was "Starry Night." My date and I socialized with friends and danced to a few songs. By "danced," I mean we held hands and gently swung our arms from side to side. While the homecoming dance was enjoyable, it was radically different from my prom experience.

Dancing with the King

Having good memories from the homecoming dance, I wanted to attend the prom despite not having a date. I decided to ask two friends if they would accompany me, and they said yes.

Early in the evening on May 1, 2004, my friends came to my house, where we kicked off Prom Night with a Chinese dinner. I never lost my taste for this cuisine since the eve of my birth. Then, Mom, who served as a chaperone along with Dad, drove us to the Maxwell C. King Center for the Performing Arts, which hosts various shows, dances, and other special events. The theme of the prom was "A Moment in Time." The dance hall was decorated with black and teal balloons and streamers. Seated at a table covered by a white tablecloth, my friends and I drank punch, chatted with classmates, and danced during a few songs.

A couple of hours later, my friends and I heard it was time for the prom king and queen to be announced, so we proceeded to the back of the dance hall. What happened next astounded me: I heard my name announced as the prom queen.

There was loud applause and cheering as my friends cleared a path for me through the crowd of students. The previous year's prom king presented me with a white sash that matched my dress, a tiara encrusted with cubic zirconium, and a silver foot-long wand matching my braces.

The teacher who was our class sponsor gave me a bouquet of roses. The prom king was a school football player whom I didn't know. We awkwardly danced to a song together. This was truly a surreal "moment in time" for me.

Prom Night is unquestionably one of the most memorable nights of my life. It made me realize my classmates had a lot of respect for me despite my disabilities. I'll always be grateful to my high school classmates for this touching gesture.

Other Senior Year Highlights

As an active FCA member throughout high school, one of my favorite senior year events was the Baccalaureate, which Mom volunteered to coordinate. This event, held at a church in Melbourne, consisted of prayer, Bible readings by students including myself, candle lighting, hymns, a baby photo flashback presentation, and speeches delivered by Palm Bay City Councilman Ken Greene and Mr. Tucker, a youth pastor at his church. I'm grateful my classmates and I had the opportunity to express our faith and give thanks for helping us get through high school.

During the last month of school, many of my classmates and I went to Islands of Adventure in Orlando to participate in Grad Bash along with other central Florida high schools. For that night, the park was closed to the public, so we had it all to ourselves and our chaperones. Some of the students rode rides while others hung out at the arcade. I beat one of the school deans at Pac-Man™, a game I had been playing since my Nintendo™ days. Grad Bash was a fun night that allowed my classmates and me to reconnect with our childhood one more time before becoming adults.

During an awards ceremony before graduation, I was pleasantly surprised to receive a scholarship from the Coca-Cola™ Bottling Group. I was recognized along with four other students for graduating with a 4.0 GPA.

My parents, all four of my grandparents, and Mrs. Pappas attended my high school graduation in May of 2004. After my name was called, I received a standing ovation as I made my way across stage shaking the hands of dignitaries, including the Palm Bay mayor, who had recently presented me with the city's first college scholarship.

A few hours after commencement, I participated in Project Graduation, a celebration for Bayside graduates, at Andretti Thrill Park in Melbourne. I played a few holes of miniature golf before encountering stairs that cut short my game. Then I cheered on my fellow graduates as they rode race cars around the track. The speed of the race cars resembled how quickly four years of high school went by for me. I was ready to move on from Bayside with memories and lessons I hope to never forget.

To celebrate my graduation, my parents threw me a party, which I referred to as "Ash Bash '04," where Aunt Bonnie lived south of Buffalo in early July. Photo collages and school memorabilia were on display. Family members and I visited with each other, watched the kids and a few adults in the pool, played games, and ate a dinner fit for a queen and cake. Everyone was invited to wish me well and give advice to be recorded for a video given to me later. The video is a gift I'll always treasure. The celebration didn't end there because the next day was my cousin Beau's sixteenth birthday.

One of my most meaningful photos from my senior yearbook is labeled "Most Likely to Succeed," which my classmates had voted me along with a male classmate. In the photo, my classmate and I are holding paper money, a sign of success. I'm flattered my fellow seniors thought of me this way, but I now believe in a different definition of success as stated by Booker T. Washington:

"I have learned that success is to be measured not so much by the position that one has reached in life as by the obstacles which he has overcome while trying to succeed."

Chapter 7

Little Woman on Campus

"I was glad to have an explanation for the way I was feeling and to know I wasn't alone in how I felt."

During an eventful hurricane season in the fall of 2004, I returned to Brevard Community College (BCC) as a full-time student with the intent to major in Accounting. In addition to core classes, I took electives related to my major such as Economics and Business Law as well as Financial Accounting. By the end of my time at BCC, I realized accounting wasn't a good fit for me professionally, so I selected a different major before moving on to my Bachelor degree. During this period, several other events took place, such as joining a prestigious organization and receiving accolades for academic excellence and community involvement.

College Students with Disabilities 101

I attended classes at the Palm Bay and Melbourne campuses while receiving services from BCC's Office for Students with disABILITIES (OSD). Due to her visual impairment, the disability services specialist at the Palm Bay campus had a service dog that served as a mascot for the OSD.

Several accommodations were made for me, including extended time on exams since I took longer to write my answers than my classmates needed. I was also given the option of typing responses to essay questions, and my professors wore a microphone that amplified their voice into my hearing aid during class lectures.

I took online courses through BCC's virtual campus, which I found to be an interesting experience. I loved how I could attend the online classes in the comfort of my bedroom whenever I wanted. This flexibility made life for me as a college student with disabilities easier and saved my parents from having to drive me to and from school for all of my classes. Despite my preference for online classes, I also enjoyed attending face-to-face classes for the sake of social interaction.

I'm grateful I had the opportunity to go to college. With a positive attitude and a focus on studying, it is possible for students with disabilities to pursue higher education. With my determination to be as independent as possible, I had to remind myself that it's okay to ask for help and to accept offers of assistance. Not only is there a disability office at the college that provides services, but there's also a financial aid office for students who may not be able to afford college. Having a college degree increases the chances of a person with disabilities of getting a job in a competitive market.

Voting with Vim and Vigor

For as long as I can remember, my parents voted in elections, so I wanted to do the same. Just a few months after registering to vote at age eighteen, I had the opportunity to exercise this right. I had learned at school about the women's suffrage movement and everything women endured to obtain their right to vote. Keeping this in mind, I always vote because voting is one way I can contribute to society as a woman with disabilities. I'm thankful for my right to vote and plan to exercise it for as long as I live.

For the presidential primaries in August, Mom and I went to Palm Bay City Hall after breakfast (Dad voted after work), and we prepared ourselves to wait in line. It wasn't too long before a campaign worker noticed Mom and me waiting outside and allowed us to go to the front of the line. I wouldn't have minded waiting until it was my turn, but that was thoughtful of the campaign worker to let me in quickly. Mom and I went inside the council chambers, where I noticed a few people from our church volunteering.

We got in line, signed in, and received our ballots. I placed myself in front of a handicapped accessible voting booth. Mom filled out her ballot in a different booth and waited for me to complete mine. We inserted our ballots into the ballot tracking machine and were given "I Voted!" stickers to put on our shirts. Mom and I went through a similar process on Election Day in November, but it was more crowded then.

Wheelchair Millionaire Wannabe

My favorite game show is *Who Wants to Be a Millionaire?* During my first semester at BCC, it was announced *Millionaire* was holding auditions for college students in New York City on November 11 (Veterans Day). I wanted to try out for the show, even though it meant a lot of arrangements had to be made in less than two weeks. Mom and Dad supported me because they knew it would be a fun experience. Mom quickly booked our flights and hotel reservations and accompanied me on the trip.

We flew to New York City the day before the audition, which caused me to miss one statistics class meeting, the only class I ever missed while attending BCC. When leaving the LaGuardia Airport, I saw a chauffeur holding a sign for Campbell Brown, who was co-anchor of *Weekend Today* at the time. I watched for celebrities but didn't see Campbell or anyone else famous. Mom and I took a handicapped accessible shuttle bus to our hotel with Central Park visible from our seats.

I would've liked to take my power chair to New York City, but it's just as well I didn't because our hotel's entrance contained stairs which my chair couldn't navigate. The hotel was about a mile from the *Millionaire* studio, so Mom pushed me in my manual wheelchair to the audition site during the afternoon of November 11. We waited outside in line with at least 100 other anxious people for well over an hour. I noticed no other community college student besides me in line, but I tried not to let that discourage me.

Eventually, the audition coordinator opened the front doors and told us we had to go to the other side of the building to take our tests. A collective groan could be heard, especially from Mom who definitely got her exercise for the day.

Finally, we were able to sign in and take our seats. The coordinator told everyone the rules for the 30-question multiple choice test, which we had ten minutes to complete. I take written tests more slowly than most people due to my fine hand motor skills, so I didn't have time to read all of the questions. When the coordinator gave us our two-minute warning, I randomly filled in the rest of my answers, hoping to get a few more points. After the tests were graded, the coordinator announced the names of those with passing scores, who would move on to the interview phase. Sadly, my name was not called.

By the time Mom and I left the studio, it was dark outside. Nervous about our unfamiliar surroundings, Mom pushed me as quickly as she could through the streets of New York City to our hotel, where we ordered room service and talked about the day we had. I felt disappointed about not passing the *Millionaire* test and guilty for asking Mom to take me to New York City for nothing.

However, I'm glad I had this opportunity because if I hadn't tried, I would've always wondered if I could achieve this goal. My dream of being a "wheelchair millionaire" didn't come true in November of 2004 or when

I took the *Millionaire* test again in Tampa (much closer to home) a few years later. I know I still have time to make it happen like the protagonist of the 2008 Academy Award-winning movie *Slumdog Millionaire*.

Going International

Grandma wanted to have another family vacation but this time closer to home. We traveled from Buffalo two hours north to Toronto, Canada, for a long weekend in July of 2005. While in Toronto, my family and I did some sightseeing, took a boat ride, went out to eat, and reunited every night in my grandparents' spacious hotel room. Since I was nineteen at the time and therefore old enough to drink alcohol legally in Canada, I took a sip out of several relatives' drinks throughout the weekend for the sake of experimentation. I found out I prefer sweeter drinks like a strawberry margarita.

I enjoyed my sojourn in Toronto. Canada is the only foreign country to which I've traveled. Since then, I applied for and have received a passport.

Phi Fun

Phi Theta Kappa (PTK) sounds like the name of a sorority, but it's actually an academic honor society for community college students comparable to Phi Beta Kappa for Bachelor degree students. There were a few requirements for membership, which I fulfilled by my second semester at BCC. Eventually, I was elected Vice President of Scholarship of the chapter at the Melbourne campus.

As a chapter officer, I attended a state PTK conference in Orlando with other members. I assisted in a couple of ceremonies during which new members were inducted. I even arranged for a state senator, who was a BCC professor, to be our guest speaker.

My fellow PTK members and I participated in the American Cancer Society's Relay for Life in Melbourne. Our team name was the Freedom Fighters, and we wore uniform T-shirts and green Statue of Liberty crowns. We were voted "Best Costume." I was presented with a green Star Supporter T-shirt for raising $1,500. Relay for Life reminded me of the importance of helping others.

In the fall of 2005, I was nominated by the chapter's sponsor to be a member of the All-USA Academic Team, a list of excellent students from all fifty states. After filling out a lengthy application, I was accepted.

A few months later, my academic teammates and I attended an awards ceremony in Tallahassee, where we received medallions and were treated to dinner by BCC's late president Dr. Thomas Gamble.

The next day happened to be my twentieth birthday. The students representing BCC were prepared for a celebratory day with party favors and a card with their signatures for me. We listened to the lieutenant governor speak and took a tour of the state Capitol building where April 6, 2006, was declared "Phi Theta Kappa Day" in Florida. These events made my twentieth birthday unforgettable.

I also volunteered at school events, such as welcome back days. At one of these events, I won tickets to an Irish concert at the King Center. Dad and I attended the show where I saw a man playing an Irish drum called the bodhran. I'm musically challenged, but I thought I could potentially play this instrument. I purchased one for myself along with a beginner's DVD with some of my BCC graduation money. Within a few months, I learned the basics. Playing the bodhran has been an entertaining way to affirm my heritage, especially with my Aunt Carol who plays the bagpipes.

During the winter break in Buffalo, Mom's family threw a party in honor of Nana and Papa's fiftieth anniversary. The celebration was held at a restaurant down the street from the church where my parents married. Nana and Papa were overjoyed with the surprises throughout the evening, along with the good food and company.

The Not-So-Great Depression

What I reveal in this section is something about myself I've told only a select few. I'm now sharing it publicly in the hopes other college students and their families will be informed by my experience.

On Labor Day of 2005, I woke up with an unusual feeling of gloom and anxiety. At first, I thought it was just because I was stressed out about a Humanities project, due in two days and worth a large percentage of my final grade. I felt temporarily better after completing my project and getting an A on it.

However, later in the semester, those unusual feelings returned. It was more difficult for me to concentrate on my schoolwork because my mind was foggy. Nana noticed I was quieter than normal during my visits with her and Papa.

After my morose mood was brought to Mom and Dad's attention, I went to therapy for the first time in a decade. I filled out a symptoms checklist, and my therapist (who had helped me get through my panic attacks ten years earlier) diagnosed me with clinical depression. I learned this was a common issue among college students for a variety of reasons such as academic pressures.

Although this didn't make me feel better overnight, I was glad to have an explanation for the way I was feeling and to know I wasn't alone in how I felt. I continued going to therapy, and by the end of the semester, I felt more like my old self again, for the time being.

I also came to the realization I was depressed partly because I was no longer interested in accounting as a career. For the final semester, I decided to enroll in an online career exploration course where I took aptitude tests and learned more about my interests and potential fields of study. For my class project, I volunteered for three months in the spring as a receptionist at my hometown's Chamber of Commerce, which I enjoyed. By the end of the course, I made a plan to major in Sociology after graduating from BCC.

Getting with the Program(s)

Because I liked to be challenged, I decided to enroll in BCC's Honors Program. Thus, I took a few honors courses and volunteered hours of community service. Eventually promoted to provost of the Cocoa campus, the program coordinator was my Communications II professor Beverly Slaughter at the Melbourne campus.

Don't let her surname scare you, she is one of the most pleasant women I know. Among other individuals, Provost Slaughter, a University of Central Florida (UCF) alumna, encouraged me to continue my education at UCF. At BCC's graduation, I received a medallion for completing the Honors Program. A photo was taken of Provost Slaughter with Honors Program graduates including myself. This Kodak™ moment was featured on the cover of the BCC Honors Program brochure.

Service learning is a program in which college students volunteer at locations that are related to their majors. I was introduced to this program in my Honors Community Involvement course. My classmates and I volunteered at places that promoted literacy.

For our class project, we, decked out in costumes, read storybooks to children at the local library. While wearing a snout mask and a pink outfit,

I read "The Three Little Pigs." My professor had the best costume in our group, for she was dressed as a hen since she read "The Little Red Hen" to the kids. This project was a fun way to serve others.

Service learning was a major component of the Citizen Scholars Program at BCC. For this program, I had to volunteer 300 hours. I started volunteering as a literacy tutor at a local library and as a BCC math tutor. I also volunteered at my church, school functions, and community events. I was required to record my service learning experiences in a journal and write a comprehensive essay at the end of the program. I received a medallion for being a Citizen Scholar and was featured on the cover of the BCC service learning brochure. The value of volunteering is one of the lessons that were reinforced for me at BCC.

The President's Cup

The most prestigious award a BCC student could receive was the President's Cup, which I was honored to receive from Dr. Gamble before his passing in 2006. My speech professor Dr. Nancy Arnett, now retired, nominated me for this award. I was flattered by the following quote from Dr. Arnett: "Her personality, sense of humor, and disposition never fail to brighten everyone's day. I cannot think of a student who has had more impact on me as an instructor than Ashley."

Words can't describe my excitement when one of BCC's vice presidents called to inform me of the wonderful news. I was the student guest speaker at the commencement at which my parents, four grandparents, and Uncle Jim sat in the front row. Several teachers and other people from my past also attended to support me. I had the privilege of sitting on stage with the faculty and administration. I spoke at two graduation ceremonies held at the King Center that day, but I didn't mind because I received standing ovations. My family and I attended a reception for the graduates following the first ceremony, where I was reunited with my guests.

Coincidentally, later that night, the 2000 movie *Remember the Titans* was on television. BCC's athletic teams were referred to as the Titans.

Chapter 8

Once a Knight, Always a Knight

"I received the worst news of my academic career."

I mentioned in a previous chapter the students at the elementary school I attended (Lockmar) are referred to as the Knights. The students at the University of Central Florida (UCF) in Orlando are also known as the Knights. Additionally, the last name of my great Aunt Rose is Knight. My life is full of Knights!

BCC + UCF = BA

In Florida, community college students have the opportunity to transfer to a public state university after completing their Associate degree. This is the path I took, which turned out to be a good one.

Because I changed my major to ˋSociology at the end of my final semester at BCC, I was required to take two introductory courses before entering the Sociology Bachelor of Arts (BA) program. Fortunately, I was able to take these classes online through BCC during the summer semester after my graduation, which prevented me from being behind in my coursework in the fall.

For the remainder of my undergraduate program, I was able to take courses in Palm Bay and Cocoa in my county, as well as online, so the commute was more tolerable. Through UCF's Student Disability Services, classmates in a few of my courses were hired to be my note-takers. I was also allowed extra time to take exams. In addition to my sociology degree, I obtained a minor in Psychology and a certificate in Women's Studies.

In the summer of 2006, my church's Society of St. Vincent de Paul food pantry announced they were in need of volunteers at their new office. One type of volunteer they asked for was data entry clerks. Although I had no experience with data entry, I thought I could help in this way since I was familiar with how to use certain computer programs.

After being trained in the data entry computer program, I began volunteering for a couple of hours per week at the food pantry. While learning a new skill, I was also reminded of how fortunate my parents and I are for never going hungry.

In the fall of 2006, I was summoned to jury duty. Apparently, physical disabilities do not exempt a person from jury duty. Thankfully, it was scheduled for the week after final exams, so I was available. In December, I reported to the local courthouse and went through security with no problems. After being questioned inside the courtroom and a lot of waiting, I wasn't selected to be a juror, but it was interesting to see the justice system in action. I was also pleased to be compensated for my time because, despite the day's low pay, this was the first time I made money.

This exposure to the courtroom experience and my desire to be an advocate led me to become a volunteer for Guardian Ad Litem. After completing training, I represented a baby whose mother had psychiatric issues. After months of home visits, progress reports, and court appearances, I was pleased to hear the judge rule in the mother's favor. As much as I enjoyed Guardian ad Litem, it required a considerable amount of driving, and due to the time demands of school, I decided not to renew my annual commitment to the program.

During my time at UCF, I was inducted into a few academic honor societies and was nominated for UCF's most prestigious student award, the Order of Pegasus. As a Psychology minor, I joined the Psychology Club at the Palm Bay campus. I served as treasurer for one semester. I attended events for UCF students in Orlando and Brevard County.

Moreover, I watched country music superstar Reba McEntire perform in the opening concert at the new UCF Arena in September of 2007. This was the first concert I'd ever attended. Although Reba looked small from where I sat in the handicapped section, I had so much fun at her concert I went to another Reba concert featuring George Strait and Lee Ann Womack at a different Orlando venue two years later.

With my parents and all four grandparents in the audience, I graduated with my BA, summa cum laude in May of 2008. At the commencement, I sat on stage once again with faculty and received a medallion for being the College of Sciences' top honor graduate. In keeping with a knightly theme, my educational credentials made me feel like a true Renaissance woman.

Nice Guys Don't Always Finish Last

Since my soft cleft palate surgery at age five, I've kept in touch with my plastic surgeon Dr. Roxanne Guy. In the spring of 2006, I was pleasantly surprised when she nominated me for a Patients of Courage award presented by the American Society of Plastic Surgeons (ASPS).

Dr. Guy, who was elected the first female ASPS president that year, thought of me for this honor as an example of someone who has led a productive life after having a birth defect corrected by reconstructive plastic surgery. An email notified me that I was selected as an award recipient and invited me to go on an all-expense paid trip to San Francisco for the annual ASPS conference in October of 2006. Dr. Guy congratulated me by ordering a bouquet of roses that were delivered to my house. An article about my award and trip was published in *The Orlando Sentinel*.

California is the furthest west from home I've ever traveled. Flying from central Florida, my parents and I had to adjust to the three-hour time difference, but the excitement we felt kept us energized during evening events. Shortly after arriving in San Francisco, I was photographed and interviewed by ASPS personnel and the local media, which made me feel like a celebrity. We attended a welcome reception at an art museum, where Dr. Guy introduced me to conference attendees. I also met and interacted with the other three award recipients: a male veteran who was injured in Iraq, a breast cancer survivor who had a mastectomy, and a woman who had complications from gastric bypass surgery.

The next night, the four of us, on stage, received glass trophies engraved with our names during an awards ceremony. The audience's standing ovation for over a minute made me feel joyful and truly accepted by others despite looking different. Moments like this serve as self-esteem boosters for me. I was impressed with how the ASPS conference presented a positive image of plastic surgery as something done for not just cosmetic reasons but also to help improve people's lives.

As if Dr. Guy and her staff didn't spoil me enough, they gave me a Celtic bracelet as a gift. Before going home, my parents and I attended Mass at St. Patrick's Church across from our Marriott hotel, explored the city (which includes a very steep street that made pushing my wheelchair nearly impossible), did some shopping (we bought a Golden Gate Bridge business card holder for Dr. Guy), and visited Union Square and Chinatown, where we ate generous helpings of delicious Chinese food. Thankfully, there wasn't an earthquake when my parents and I were in San Francisco like there was a century before. Keeping school in mind, I studied for a statistics midterm during the flight home.

I'm deeply indebted to Dr. Guy for everything she did for me throughout my life. I don't believe the saying "nice guys finish last" applies to her, and she is the nicest Guy I know.

A Very Good Friday

My twenty-first birthday in 2007 happened to fall on Good Friday, two days before Easter. Since my family and I were preparing for the most important day of the year for Catholics and other Christians, the official celebration of my birthday was postponed for a week. It was definitely worth the wait because my parents threw me a catered party for my birthday at my church's parish hall, which was decorated in pink.

More than 100 people attended, including my four grandparents, Uncle Bobby, and my youngest cousin Madison from western New York, and the Mayor of Palm Bay. A DJ I knew from church provided the entertainment and many people danced the night away. A local Irish duet played a set with a fiddle and a guitar; I played my bodhran during the song "Lord of the Dance" after weeks of practice.

The celebration of my twenty-first birthday made me feel extra special. Grandpa summed it up, saying, "This is the best birthday party I ever went to."

My parents and other people have referred to me as a "star" over the years due to my brightness and efforts to pursue my dreams. Therefore, I find it fitting that, for my twenty-second birthday, Mom and Dad bought me a star in the sky through the International Star Registry. They presented me with a certificate on which my star number is printed. This was a unique gift I appreciated. I'm not superstitious, but it's nice to know I have a star upon which to wish.

Another New York Side Trip

In July of 2008, Dad's family was ready for another vacation, so we rented a home in Ellicottville, New York. The area in which we stayed for almost a week was beautiful. The sunrise woke me up before 6:00 every morning like clockwork. I didn't mind getting up early too much because I was ready to start my day with the family. Throughout the week, we played games like Scrabble™ and bocce, celebrated Aunt Kathie's fiftieth birthday with a cake, went to church, and explored the local area. I had planned to go fishing with my Uncle George, but I found out I needed a fishing license in the state of New York, so we ended up at a casino where we played blackjack. As usual, I was sad to see our family vacation end but felt grateful for new happy memories.

Mastering Graduate School

A few months before graduating from UCF, I received a letter from the Department of Sociology inviting me to enroll in their Applied Sociology Master of Arts (MA) program starting in the fall. As much as I liked school, I'd planned to try to get a job after graduation, but a few of my professors recommended I pursue my Master's in order to have more career opportunities. I knew Dad and Papa had Master's degrees, so I didn't think it would hurt to try. After some serious consideration, I filled out the application and was accepted in the MA program.

Shortly before starting my Master's, I finally got my ears pierced at age twenty-two. I decided to do this after watching my cousin Tess get her third ear piercing without batting an eye. I waited so long to do it because I was afraid it was going to hurt. A few people thought this was silly considering all of the surgeries I underwent. Looking back, I think it was silly, too, because it hurt tolerably for only a few minutes. I'm glad I got my ears pierced because it makes me look a little more feminine while having short hair.

I began the Applied Sociology MA program at UCF in August of 2008. I also began my first job. After being invited by the program coordinator, I attended a training session and worked part-time as a graduate teaching assistant for one of my former sociology professors. My duties included answering students' questions as needed online and grading homework assignments and quizzes. For my services, I was given a partial tuition waiver along with my paycheck.

The first semester of graduate school was harder than I'd anticipated. I had to commute to and from the main campus in Orlando, more than 120 miles round trip, twice a week. I was so stressed out I found myself experiencing symptoms of depression again halfway through the semester. I paid a visit to my physician, who prescribed me an antidepressant, which took weeks to take effect. I didn't want my depression to have a negative impact on my GPA, so I took an incomplete for one of my classes. However, I managed to ace the other two classes I took.

A group called Ladies' Night Out with a Purpose, founded by my family friend Trish in September 2008, provided a fun distraction from studies. Mom and I met with the women once a month to socialize and play games. Members made a monthly donation that went to a local charity. Six years later, we still meet and enjoy our friendship.

In December of 2008, my parents and I attended a taping of *Wheel of Fortune*, another favorite game show of mine, at SeaWorld. From where I sat, Pat Sajak and Vanna White looked small, but I was able to watch the show on a screen. It was neat to see the set with the puzzle board and the big wheel. Since we were at SeaWorld, a seal was in the audience clapping like everybody else. Someday, I want to take my wheels to *Wheel* as a contestant.

After winter break, I decided to take a special leave of absence for one semester. Thankfully, UCF's Department of Sociology and my family were understanding about my situation.

Depression was worse for me the second time around, which is common for relapses. I understand what figure skater Scott Hamilton meant when he said the only disability in life is a bad attitude. Being severely depressed made me feel even more disabled.

Before going back to counseling, I saw a psychiatrist, who continued to prescribe me the medication my primary care physician started for me. Then, I met my therapist Linda, who happens to be from Angola, New York, where my mom lived for part of her childhood. Over time, the combination of medication and counseling helped me significantly.

Within a couple of months, I finished the coursework for my incomplete class, which I ended up acing. With my birthday money, I bought myself a netbook computer in April of 2009. Finally, I felt ready to go back to school, so I signed up for two summer courses, both of which I aced. I also did well with the classes I took in the fall. I was grateful for feeling motivated again for the foreseeable future.

My Vegas Vacation

In the spring of 2009, I took up a new hobby: No-Limit Texas Hold'em Poker. I had been interested in this game after watching it on TV since 2003 and received a poker set from Papa and Nana shortly before my high school graduation.

Unlike more physical activities, this was something I could do sitting in a wheelchair for hours. I had played the game occasionally with relatives and at the local racetrack, but this was the first time I played poker in a public setting on a regular basis. Under proper management league poker is legal because no gambling actually takes place since no money is wagered; play money chips are used during league poker games. Players are only asked to give dealers a tip. After winning a game, a player qualifies for the seasonal league championship. The more wins the player accumulates during a season, the more chips he or she starts with at the championship.

I started playing poker through a league at a local coffeehouse. After the league shut down within a month due to lack of players, I joined two other area leagues where I played games at local restaurants and other venues. After a couple of years, I decided to play in just one league to maximize my number of wins. This was a good move for me because I placed in the top ten out of about 500 people at two consecutive championships in 2012 for which I received plaques and silver-plated coins.

In June of 2009, I flew with my parents to Las Vegas to compete in the ladies' event of the 40th annual World Series of Poker (WSOP) at the Rio Hotel & Casino. Despite being in "Sin City," my parents and I attended Mass at a local church the day before the ladies' tournament. On the day of the event, I proudly wore my poker league shirt along with sunglasses and a UCF visor, which are common accessories for poker players. About an hour after the tournament began, I was astonished when Daniel Negreanu, one of my favorite professional poker players, came to my table and called out my name. He asked me how I was doing and touched my poker chips.

"Get pocket aces or something," said Daniel, referring to the best starting hand in hold'em, before he returned to his tournament.

Shortly after that, I won a hand with pocket kings, a pair of kings dealt to me facedown, and hoped the good luck would continue.

Unfortunately, I only lasted a few hours in the tournament. Mom likes to say, in a teasing manner, our flight lasted longer than my game. However, I still had an awesome week. I saw Daniel a few more times and met and received autographs from other professional poker players, including the legendary Doyle Brunson and *Celebrity Apprentice* runner-up Annie Duke.

It was surreal for me to see all of these poker players I had watched on TV for years. I also met Penn and Teller after watching one of their magic shows at the Rio. During my photo opportunity with Penn, who is quite tall, he said, "Here, let me get down to human size."

On the other hand, Teller, who doesn't speak during his act, gave me the silent treatment. I also did some sightseeing in Las Vegas, which included going to the top of the Paris Hotel's replica of the Eiffel Tower with Dad. I submitted a letter about my WSOP experience to the editors of the poker magazine *Ante Up*, and it was published later in the summer. Mom compiled two albums of my photos, autographs, and other memorabilia. My family and fellow league players enjoyed hearing about my week at the WSOP.

From Disappointment to Accomplishment

Depression returned once again in the spring of 2010 due to a series of unfortunate events. In January, I quit taking my antidepressant after consulting with my psychiatrist because I felt so much better and didn't think I needed it anymore (bad idea).

A few days later, I found out my class schedule wouldn't allow me to go on my first cruise in April with my parents and fellow churchgoers that was planned the year before. This really disappointed me and made me feel guilty since my parents had already paid their non-refundable deposit.

Later in January, I noticed itchy and oozing rashes on my legs, which, in hindsight, was probably a sign of extreme stress. I was nominated once again for UCF's Order of Pegasus only to find out in February my application was rejected for the second time. The sadness from this rejection pales in comparison to what happened next.

In March, I received the worst news of my academic career: I failed the Applied Sociology MA comprehensive exam, so I wouldn't graduate with my classmates in the spring. This setback truly shocked and devastated me.

For the sake of my coursework and group project, I did what was necessary to complete the semester with A's in April. Around the same time, Dad had a bicycling accident and underwent surgery to repair a broken collarbone. He had to wear a sling, which meant he was unable to carry me for a few weeks. Although he recovered quickly, seeing Dad injured had an effect on me. Dad's medical situation combined with knowing I wouldn't graduate on time led me further into depression.

I went back onto my antidepressant and went to therapy more frequently. The only thing that stood in the way of my Master's degree was the comprehensive exam. Although I really didn't want to, I retook the exam in June and passed it, thanks to professors' feedback and my parents' encouragement.

I graduated in August of 2010, just three months later than originally planned. This doesn't seem so terrible in the whole scheme of things, but as someone who prided myself on academic excellence, this experience was deflating for me.

One highlight of 2010 for me was reading a passage from the Bible at my friend Alana's wedding in June. I've known Alana and her family from school and church since I was five years old; I fondly recall dancing with Alana's mother Trish at a church volunteer appreciation dinner back then and again at my twenty-first birthday party. So, I felt honored to be a part of Alana and her husband Ryan's special day. Their reception in the church hall was catered by the same people who catered my twenty-first birthday party. This event provided me with a day of joy during my period of depression that summer.

I've learned while certain factors such as heredity and stress levels elevate the probability of occurrence, depression can hit anybody at any time. People with this condition need to know they can live a good life with counseling, the right combination of medications (if necessary), and the support of family and friends. I'm a living example of this.

Chapter 9

No Pressure (OK, Maybe a Little)

"Mom thought I was playing a joke on her."

Graduating with my Master's degree was one of the best accomplishments of my life, but the positive feedback from this achievement didn't last long. Before I knew it, I was being encouraged to find a job when I just wanted to relax and have some fun for a little while after going to school for over fifteen years.

I went to Vocational Rehabilitation (VR), an organization that helps people with disabilities become employed. I had a consultation with a job coach assigned to me by VR, but I didn't actively look for work in the fall of 2010. I truly felt I needed a break not because I was lazy or scared about joining the workforce; there was a deeper underlying reason I couldn't explain.

I attended individual as well as family counseling in an effort to deal with my feelings. Apparently, I should've listened to my body, for I experienced negative effects of extreme stress from everything that happened in the first half of 2010.

In the Days Before . . .

During the afternoon of Monday, December 13, 2010, Mom and I were chatting, and she asked me a few simple questions I had trouble answering. Concerned this may be a psychological issue, Mom called my therapist Linda and put me on the phone so she could hear how I talked. I have no recollection of my phone conversation with Linda.

The following night, Mom and I met Dad and Uncle Jim, who was in Brevard County for business, at a seafood restaurant in Cocoa Beach. On the way to the restaurant, Mom and I had the following conversation:

"This is nice, Mom," I said. "Where are we going?"

"What do you mean, where are we going?" Mom replied in a surprised tone. "We're going to the Lobster Shanty to meet Dad and Uncle Jim for dinner."

"Uncle Jim is in town?" I said. "Cool! It's been a while since I've seen him."

Mom glanced at me with a puzzled look and continued driving. A couple of minutes later, Mom and I exchanged similar words. At this point, Mom thought I was playing a joke on her. After having the same conversation for the third time, she realized I really couldn't remember what she told me just two minutes ago. I sounded like a broken record.

We finally made it to the restaurant, where I proceeded to sample foods I normally dislike such as coleslaw and dessert with whipped cream. Otherwise, my behavior during dinner was socially acceptable. On the way home, I acted paranoid about being on the road in the dark. Mom kept reassuring me everything was okay, Dad was following us, and we would be home soon.

The next day, Mom took me to my primary care doctor and told her about my strange behavior from the past couple of days. As a test, the doctor asked me a few questions about going out for dinner the night before. She soon realized there was something off about me. The nurse checked my blood pressure, which was higher than usual. Unsure of what to make of my condition, my doctor advised me to get some rest and just take it easy.

My Last Trip to the ER

During the morning of Thursday, December 16, Mom and I were trying to play a card game when she realized something was drastically wrong with me. I was speaking strangely, having trouble making decisions, and not acting like myself, so Mom called Uncle John, a psychological researcher, and told him about my strange behavior and speech. I spoke with Uncle John on the phone, and then, he advised Mom to take me to the hospital for testing.

This was an inconvenient time for me to be acting like this since we were about to travel to western New York for the holidays. To be on the safe side, Mom called Dad at work, and they decided to take me to the emergency room at the hospital in Palm Bay. My blood pressure was checked, and it was sky high. I was admitted into the hospital where I remained for five days.

Along with Nana and Papa, several people from my church came to visit and prayed with me in the hospital. I received flowers, numerous get-well cards, and phone calls from people out of town. I appreciated the outpouring of support.

I underwent a battery of tests, but doctors at the hospital weren't completely sure what was wrong with me. I felt like a patient with confusing symptoms on the show *House* (2004-2012). The doctors' best guess was hypertension, which could've led to short-term memory loss.

For Christmas in 2010, I wanted an iPod Touch™. My parents gave it to me early before our scheduled travel. Evidently, my delirium led me to forget about it because after seeing an ad for the iPod Touch™ in the hospital, I asked Mom if I could have one for Christmas. She retrieved my iPod from my bag and showed it to me. Feeling foolish, I realized Mom and Dad had already given me an iPod.

During my hospitalization, I kept asking my parents why I was in the hospital, and they kept trying to explain, but I didn't comprehend what they told me. At one point, Mom became emotional and hurried into the bathroom.

"Is Mom okay?" I asked Dad, looking up from my hospital bed.

"Mom's fine, honey," said Dad. "She's just concerned about you."

I returned to my constant questioning.

Under doctors' orders, I tried a few different medications to manage my hypertension. After finding a blood pressure medication to which I responded well, I was discharged from the hospital and spent the holidays with my parents, maternal grandparents, and friends close to home. Although I missed being with family in western New York, I still had a merry Christmas. We used Skype™ on my computer to talk with my relatives up north during the holidays, so it was almost like being in the same room with them.

A Different Kind of Recovery

January of 2011 was about rest and relaxation, getting back to a normal routine, and finding myself again. I had follow-ups with a few of my doctors. Measuring it regularly with a monitor at home, my blood pressure eventually came back down to normal, and my short-term memory improved significantly within a few weeks of my hospitalization. I made sure not to take on too much too soon, and my parents understood this. However, I couldn't just sit around all day and do nothing. I still had to find a job and put my Master's degree to good use.

In February, I received an email from a friend about a writing website that pays article writers. Shortly thereafter, I obtained the position of Orlando Special Needs Kids Examiner for Examiner.com. This consisted of writing two articles per week about issues that are relevant to special needs kids and their families in the Orlando area. I didn't make much money for doing this, but it gave me exposure and experience as a writer. I felt proud of my writing because the information I provided seemed to be beneficial to my readers.

After becoming an Examiner, I learned from my job coach about a tutoring opportunity. I did so well during the interview I was hired on the spot by a non-profit organization that provides services to children with and without disabilities in Brevard County.

Following a background check, I served as a math tutor for high school students. This was a rewarding job in which I felt productive and helpful, and the hourly rate for tutors wasn't too shabby. Not long after I was hired, I attended a dinner/awards reception that displayed the impact of the tutoring company on the community.

Having these two part-time jobs made me feel better about myself. I felt more like an adult.

However, at the same time, I showed signs of hypomania, a state characterized by untiringly elevated and irritable moods. Besides being overly happy, I talked incessantly, found a way to keep myself occupied at all times, expressed my frustration to my parents more often, and slept fewer hours. Building on my creative energy, I created a sit-down comedy act I took to Orlando where I auditioned for a talent company in early 2011. I also performed twice at a local hotel. My goal of becoming famous was short-lived, but it was still a fun experience.

I spent the evening of my twenty-fifth birthday eating dinner with my family and playing poker with friends at a local pizzeria. Shortly after that, I competed at a World Poker Tour (WPT) tournament at the Hard Rock Hotel & Casino in Hollywood, Florida. Although I didn't win money, I enjoyed myself.

My parents were glad I wasn't severely depressed anymore, but they feared my extreme excitability wasn't healthy, either. Dealing with me in my hypomanic state was almost as challenging for them as taking care of me during recovery from surgery. My parents knew something had to be done to bring me back to a sense of normalcy.

In April of 2011, we went to my psychiatrist, who changed my diagnosis from major depressive disorder to bipolar II disorder. She added a mood enhancer to be taken with my antidepressant. The new medicine calmed me down so much it made me sleepy during the day and early in the evening, but it appeared to control my mood swings. Throughout the spring and summer, the dosages of my medications were changed in an attempt to find a healthy balance, and that was easier said than done.

Going South

Although my parents have lived in Florida since before I was born, they hadn't been to Key West. We found out Uncle John was going to Key West to visit friends for Memorial Day weekend in 2011. My parents and I decided we would meet him there. Taking the holiday traffic into consideration, it took us about seven hours to drive from Palm Bay to Key West.

The long drive was worth it. My parents and I ate dinner at the original Jimmy Buffett's Margaritaville Café and watched the sunset at Mallory Square. The next day, we ate lunch and visited with Uncle John at a restaurant near our hotel.

On Memorial Day, we went to Ernest Hemingway's house where numerous cats roam the property. I had a staring contest with one of the cats, and the cat won. I wasn't able to go upstairs like other visitors because of my wheelchair. I read a couple of Hemingway's books in high school, so it was interesting to see where one of the most famous American authors lived.

We also went to a butterfly sanctuary, where butterflies perched on Dad and me, and the site of the southernmost point in the United States. Mom ate more than her fair share of key lime pie during the weekend.

The scenery and atmosphere of Key West, also known as the Conch Republic, made me feel like I was in a different country. Despite the drowsiness from my medications, going to the southern end of the United States was fun.

Back to the Drawing Board

Almost five months had passed since my successful interview with the tutoring company in March of 2011 without my being assigned to a student, so I was advised to seek another part-time job while waiting for my first student. In early August, I decided to interview for a part-time position at the BCC Melbourne campus's Office for Students with disABILITIES. I felt confident because I was familiar with this office since I received services from it. Unfortunately, the interview didn't go as well as I would've liked. Having put a lot of pressure on myself, I was so disappointed I immediately began having overly negative thoughts associated with depression.

Two days later, my parents and I started our road trip to western New York. A couple of days after arriving in the Buffalo area, we drove for two hours to Keuka Lake, one of the Finger Lakes, where Dad's family was staying at a vacation home. Due to my rapidly worsening depression, the fun factor in this family vacation wasn't there for me, and Uncle John noticed this.

After returning to my grandparents' house from the Finger Lakes, my parents had my antidepressants, which I hadn't been taking for a few months, refilled at the pharmacy. During the next month-and-a-half, it became increasingly harder for me to control my thoughts and mood. I felt even more miserable than Winnie-the-Pooh's friend Eeyore. My parents, psychiatrist, and therapist all assured me this, too, would pass, but I wasn't convinced. By the end of September, I begged Mom to have me hospitalized in the psych ward because I was so desperate and felt more needed to be done to preserve my sanity.

During an emergency session with my parents and therapist present, my psychiatrist prescribed a stimulant to go with my antidepressant and mood enhancer in an effort to boost my energy level. I took the stimulant for a couple of weeks but was still not satisfied with how I felt, so my psychiatrist added a low dosage of lithium, a mood stabilizer, to my regimen. However, I now needed blood work done to monitor lithium levels to prevent toxicity.

In November, I showed signs of delirium once again, and my parents wanted to get a second opinion on how to manage my bipolar disorder. Mom called a friend from our church who was a licensed clinical social worker. She helped us set up an appointment with the psychiatrist with whom she works.

After asking me some questions, this psychiatrist concluded I was delirious due to being overmedicated. Within a couple of weeks, I was taking only two medications instead of four for my bipolar disorder. These medications negatively affect my thyroid gland, so I take a separate medication to counteract that. I also take a hormone therapy pill and medication for gastric acid reflux.

Due to my narrow trachea and swallowing issues, medications need to be chewable, liquid, powder or suppositories.

By Christmas, I felt more mentally stable and able to enjoy life again. My process of gaining a sense of stability started a year before with my hospitalization. Finding a solution, especially in the field of mental health, takes patience and persistence. Since mental illness is a lifelong issue, solutions are not simply a quick fix. To maintain good mental health years later, I continue to take my medications and visit my therapist and psychiatrist every so often.

In total, I have more than a dozen doctors to visit every year. Mom refers to me as a "patient patient."

My parents and I could tell with the passing of time, I was getting better. I was able to work as a tutor for the rest of the school year. I lost my job in August of 2012 due to the tutoring company's downsizing, and although I was bummed briefly, I didn't fall apart.

I began looking at websites with job listings and reached out to my network of contacts. In an effort to make myself more marketable, I took a teaching certification exam in the subject area of social science grades 6-12. Based on what happened with my Master's comprehensive exam, I was nervous about the possibility of failing the teaching certification exam, but I passed it on my first try and was eligible for a teaching certificate.

The relative lack of jobs for sociology graduates combined with my limited physical abilities complicated my job search, but I kept myself occupied with volunteering, writing, church activities, and my hobbies.

The following quote by Eleanor Roosevelt has served me well as an individual with disabilities and medical issues: "No one can make you feel inferior without your consent."

Going North

In August of 2012, my parents and I joined Dad's family at a vacation home by Lake Conesus in New York for a few days. We celebrated Grandpa and my cousin Sarah's birthday on August 8. For the first time since I was little, I laid on a hammock. When I wasn't outside enjoying the beautiful weather, I watched some of the Summer Olympics from Beijing, China. Before I knew it, it was time to go back to Buffalo.

After leaving the vacation home, my parents and I went to the New York side of Niagara Falls. I had gone to Niagara Falls once before as a child, but the mist from the rushing water made it difficult for me to breathe back then. The second time around, my parents pushed me in my wheelchair to the railing by the falls.

Thankfully, I was able to breathe and enjoy the view of Niagara Falls over which high-wire artist Nik Wallenda had the courage to walk on a tightrope almost two months prior to my visit. Before leaving Niagara Falls, my parents and I ate lunch at a restaurant overlooking the water and bought souvenirs at the gift shop to commemorate that day.

I went on my first cruise with my parents and members of Dad's family in October of 2013. We sailed on Royal Caribbean's Grandeur of the Seas from Baltimore to Portland, Maine, and two ports in Canada and back over an eight-day period. During our stops on land, I was amazed by the multiple colors of leaves on trees, for we don't have much of an autumn in central Florida.

In Portland, my parents and I went to the home of poet Henry Wadsworth Longfellow. Each day on the ship was filled with fun activities such as trivia, karaoke, and casino games. There were several delicious options for breakfast and lunch. Choosing from a fine dining menu, the family ate dinner together every night in the Great Gatsby ballroom. We attended a few evening shows featuring musicians, acrobatic dancers, and a comedian.

I was glad to have the chance to spend quality time with my cousin Ben, who's my age. One night, I met and had a picture taken with the ship's captain. Mom asked him, "Who's steering the ship?"

The cruise was wonderful, and I recommend it as an excellent vacation for wheelchair users. My parents and I stayed in an accessible, spacious stateroom. The friendly and attentive staff made my family feel like royalty.

The Cycle of Life

In the second half of 2012, it was clear Papa's long-term health issues were worsening, but like Nana and my parents, I hoped he would recover once again. After a couple of hospitalizations, a brief stay at a medical rehabilitation center, and one night in hospice, Papa passed away on December 18, exactly eighty years after he was baptized as an infant in the United Evangelical Church.

My parents and I still managed to take Nana to Buffalo for the holidays, which had a different tone for us. While keeping Papa in our minds and hearts, we made the best of our Christmas celebrations and family gatherings that year.

Four weeks after Papa's passing, a joyful event took place on Mom's side of the family: My cousin Kate gave birth to a boy, Daniel, named after his father. This was a historic moment in our family because Danny is

Nana's first great-grandchild. His little brother Dawson was born the following year.

These births remind me of how excited I was when my youngest cousins Madison, Ian, and Max were born. Despite living 1,200 miles away from them, I've enjoyed watching my cousins (the closest things I have to siblings) grow up over the years. I look forward to watching Danny's and Dawson's development through online photographs, video clips, Skype™ chats, and future visits.

I feel fortunate to have had Papa in my life for twenty-six years. I think about him and what I learned from him often. Although he wasn't Catholic like Nana, Papa always supported his children and grandchildren in their faith (he even came to my church whenever I did a Bible reading). As an educator devoted to his family, he was a godly man by being a positive influence for many people, myself included. For the rest of my life, I'll attempt to emulate him in this way.

Epilogue

I'm Not a Wheelchair Potato

My paternal ancestors immigrated to America from Ireland during the nineteenth and twentieth centuries. Prior to their exodus, there was a potato famine in the mid-1800s, resulting in one million deaths.

Fast forward to the year 2007 when I was preparing to deliver a speech about volunteering during a faculty in-service at Brevard Community College (BCC). Mom suggested I use the phrase *wheelchair potato* in my speech. This was a unique way to display how being active in my community prevented me from being idle in my wheelchair.

I liked the idea behind *wheelchair potato*, so I took Mom's advice and concluded my speech with those words, which were well-received by my audience. Nowadays, I continue to do my best in living up to my mantra.

Life Lessons Learned

As a young woman who has had physical disabilities her entire life, I've learned a few lessons that are also applicable to non-disabled people. I shared these lessons with my fellow BCC graduates during my commencement speech in 2006. Below are the life lessons:

- Focus on what you are able to do instead of what you are unable to do.
- Be courageous and persistent while pursuing your dreams.
- Remember you have the potential to make a positive difference in your family and your community and even your country and the world.

A common theme in my life lessons is attitude. Some people have more adversity than others, but having a positive attitude can help a person deal with personal problems. This attitude contributes to a better quality of life.

Oh, the Places I'll Go!

As a person with disabilities, I have fewer career opportunities than my able-bodied counterparts. Nevertheless, I haven't let this fact stop me from going after my dreams.

In the summer of 2014, I was hired as a quality analyst by J.Lodge Corporation, a company that employs mostly people with disabilities. Working part-time from home, I listen to recordings of phone calls between sales agents and customers, checking for rules violations and possible cases of fraud. I fill out electronic forms with necessary information obtained from the phone calls.

Whatever else I do in life, I hope to make a difference in the lives of the people I encounter.

After my high school graduation, Grandma gave me some invaluable advice all people should follow: "You have so much potential in many areas that I know you will succeed at whatever you decide is right for you. It is so important to like what you are doing for a living. My advice would be to give a lot of thought and consideration of what seems appealing to you. And then go get it."

I'm doing my best to follow Grandma's advice, and I hope you will, too.

Afterword

Ashley's Mom

Being first-time parents seemed scary enough, but bringing a newborn home with medical issues was overwhelming. That first year, I developed hives and insomnia from the stress and uncertainty. However, I was grateful to be twenty-eight years old, married to Marty for four years, and in our own home.

There are countless "best" days and memorable moments for me as Ashley's mom, but one of my "worst" days was in March of 1992. Ashley, who was five, just had spine surgery and was recovering in the pediatric intensive care unit at Minneapolis Children's Hospital, over 1,600 miles from home. She was on a respirator, in traction, with tubes and IVs everywhere. She looked so frail and was laboring for each breath. I just wanted her suffering to end.

Family members who came to be with us for her operation had to leave to go back to their lives. My husband also had to fly home and return to work. Surrounded by strangers and unable to comfort my child, I felt helpless, terrified, and exhausted. Crying and praying were the only two things I could do.

In a matter of twenty-four hours, Ashley's situation improved greatly, and so did my state of mind. Having Ashley as my daughter equipped me with courage and strength I didn't know I possessed.

The end of 2010 and most of 2011 was an emotionally draining time for us. Totally unrelated to Ashley's syndrome was witnessing our otherwise happy-go-lucky daughter becoming unhappy and questioning her existence.

Mental illness is complex and confusing, and there isn't an easy fix. Watching a loved one struggle through this illness was heartbreaking. I had to hide my tears and fears and muster all my positivity. The biggest challenge was waiting for our daughter's stability and peace to return. To finally see her smile and experience joy again was pure rapture.

Even though I wouldn't decide differently and considering how much I love and enjoy my sisters and brother, having a sibling could have been good for our daughter. I'm glad I was able to devote my undivided attention to only one child. I've made my share of mistakes and unintentionally hurt and embarrassed Ashley like any regular mother. Our relationship has been through phases from harmony to turmoil.

I still have her Christening gown and First Communion, Confirmation, and prom dresses in her closet. I've also kept her first lock of cut hair, ear tubes, rods removed from her spine, and all her baby teeth. Letting go isn't my strong suit. I know in my heart, Ashley appreciates her imperfect parents and our efforts over the years.

Two sayings that have applied to our life are "When the going gets tough, the tough get going," and "This too shall pass." Having a child with special needs was a life Marty and I were unprepared for, but it is our calling and has become a life we've learned to adapt to and live day by day (oh, dear Lord).

Ashley's Dad

On April 6, 1986, my wife Tracy and I held our newborn daughter Ashley for the first time. As I looked at her, I had such a feeling of peace and joy.

Although there were indications, we didn't know for a few months that Ashley's life would be different in many ways. I'm thankful our family has been fortunate to have good health care, live in a time of ADA awareness, and have opportunities not available in the past.

When Ashley was five years old, we traveled from Florida to Minneapolis Children's Hospital for surgery. Ashley's spine curvature was increasing rapidly, and the progression had to be stopped. Easy options were already exhausted, and as parents, Tracy and I had to make difficult decisions. Ultimately, Ashley was faced with the hardest part, which was the complex operation her spine surgeon recommended.

As Tracy and I waited at the hospital with my mom and brother John, we were left with our thoughts, prayers, and hopes that all would turn out well. We received updates during the operation and after several hours were able to see Ashley in intensive care. To me, she seemed barely alive, lying there with tubes and machines all around her.

Due to her breathing tube, Ashley couldn't talk. Years before, she had learned sign language. Now in post-op, Ashley was signing to us again. She gave a simple sign of the letter J, which indicated she wanted to see her Uncle John. I had such a sense of relief as I saw the J and knew Ashley was going to be all right.

There would be other trips to Minneapolis and more surgeries for Ashley. While medical problems had to be solved, we did some fun things, t the Mall of America, Ashley and I rode the indoor Ferris wheel and visited the Lego™ store.

Ashley and I also spent some time at the Metrodome early on the day of a Minnesota Twins game. The place was empty except for a few stadium workers, who didn't mind our roaming the halls and looking out over the baseball field from various locations. At one point, we saw a photographer taking pictures of a pizza to be shown later on the scoreboard to advertise the concession stands. Our timing was good as we passed by and were offered a free slice or two. We had fun exploring but soon returned to our hotel to get ready for Ashley's next appointment.

During her senior year at Bayside High School, Ashley and I attended all the home football games. Since the rail on the bleachers blocked her view, we were allowed to watch the games on the track surrounding the field. As the Bayside Bears moved down the field, we were able to move with them along the track. We were so close to the field that it really felt like we were a part of the action. Ashley always brought her enthusiasm and spirit to such events, and because of this, I was able to enjoy them as well.

It is said, "A journey of a thousand miles begins with a single step." I have seen Ashley's courageous steps in dealing with difficulty in her life's journey. Somehow, we have made it through the difficult days. The somehow is due to the help of God.

Ashley has overcome many challenges in her life. With support from God, family, and many others, she continues to live a life only she can live.

About the Author

Ashley M. McGrath is a quality analyst for J.Lodge Corporation and an active member of her church. Receiving numerous awards during her school years, Ashley has a Master's degree in Applied Sociology from the University of Central Florida. She serves as a board member for the Space Coast Writers' Guild and as a volunteer in her community. Although she's only twenty-eight years old, Ashley decided to write her autobiography because she has significant life experience she wanted to share with others. Ashley lives with her parents in Palm Bay, Florida.

If you have a question or would like to leave a comment, you may email Ashley at AshMarMcG@aol.com. You can also find her on LinkedIn, Facebook, and Twitter (@AshMarMcG).

Made in the USA
Monee, IL
26 December 2021

87223140R00069